Ecological
Renewal

ECOLOGICAL

RENEWAL

PAUL E. LUTZ

and

H. PAUL SANTMIRE

FORTRESS PRESS

Philadelphia

The lines on pp. 76–77 from "The Second Coming" by William Butler Yeats are reprinted with the permission of The Macmillan Company from *Collected Poems* by William Butler Yeats. Copyright 1924 by The Macmillan Company, renewed 1952 by Bertha Georgie Yeats.

Library of Congress Catalog Card Number 76-179633

ISBN 0-8006-1450-X

3159J71   Printed in U.S.A.   1-1450

Contents

Editor's Foreword

Confrontation Books aim to confront the involved reader with the cross of Christ amid the crossroads of life. Confrontations are central to Christianity: both at the cross, for the content of Christian faith, and at the crossroads, for the context of Christian love. To enable responsible men to confront both life in Christ and Christ in life is the dialectical hallmark of authentic Christian theology.

Paul sharply contrasts two opposing types of theology: that of the contemplation of heaven and that of confrontation in the world. Theology can describe either man's search for God or God's search for man. Our choice determines our method.

If man's basic problem is considered to be his ignorance as a finite creature, then knowledge of God may properly be sought through man's rational speculation. If, rather, man's essential dilemma is confessed to be his idolatry as a proud and disobedient sinner, then knowledge of God can be achieved only through God's gracious self-revelation. Paul's gospel was regarded as scandalous by the religious men of his day precisely because he rejected man-centered contemplation in the name of Christ-centered confrontation: "When the time had fully come, God sent forth his Son . . . Formerly, when you did not know God, you were in bondage to beings that by nature are not gods, but now . . . you have come to know God, or rather to be known by God" (Gal. 4: 8–9).

Ours is therefore a *theology of worldly confrontation:*

"God was in Christ reconciling the world to himself." No biblical theme is more promising for Christian renewal than the liberating gospel of God's ministry of reconciliation, grounded in Christ's cross and proclaimed by Christ's Church. In opposition to the rash of recent religious fads, the hidden lordship of the crucified Christ still constitutes the heart of the apostolic good news.

In a frightened and confused age, "Christ-figures" and "redemptive movements" rise and fall almost weekly. They pass by in dizzying succession in response to post-modern man's futile attempts to match his technological prowess in a shrinking world with some commensurate form of ideological universalism. However, the cross of the one unique Christ—Jesus of Nazareth—remains faith's unswerving answer to the institutional church's present "identity crisis:" its seeming inability to become lovingly *identified with* the world without also becoming faithlessly *identical to* the world. Our suffering theology is no substitute for God's "suffering servant." We need to recapture that paradoxical unity of universality and particularity that undergirds Paul's gospel of God's reconciling work in Jesus of Nazareth, the Second Adam, who incorporates a new humanity into a new covenant with life's Lord.

Ours is also an *ethic of worldly confrontation:* "As you did it to one of the least of these my brethren, you did it to me." Apathetic Christians need to be reminded that Christ-centered reconciliation must always be viewed in the light of God's righteousness and judgment. Christian reconciliation in an evil world has nothing to do with either non-committal neutrality or uninvolved appeasement.

Although Jesus surely died for all men, he also lived especially for some—the poor, the weak, the dispossessed, "the least of these my brethren." The Church, as the reconciling body of the risen Christ, is called to minister likewise. All men are sinners before a righteous God, but not all men are victims in an unjust society. This demands that we clearly distinguish, without falsely separating or equating, the Church and the world. Our Christian hope lies in neither the secularization of the Church nor the sacralization of the world. Rather, the Church's worldly stance must remain in evangelical tension: strictly impartial in faith as it serves all sinful men alike in its ministry of Word and sacrament, yet compassionately partial in love as it struggles on behalf of God's suffering "have-nots" in its ministry of mercy and justice.

Confrontation Books, committed to man's personal confrontation with the cross of Christ amid the crossroads of life, will engage in down-to-earth theology in fidelity to a down-to-earth Lord. Readers are invited to think theologically (in depth before God) about the actual problems of life that confront them daily.

Our age, especially, challenges Christian theology to authenticate itself by responding humanely to the host of medical, political, racial, and military threats and opportunities facing mankind. In Confrontation Books, therefore, ecumenical authors of various churches, races, nationalities, and professions will seek to develop current Christian life-styles by confronting controversial secular problems with biblical insights and theological affirmations of faith—e.g., pollution, heroin, revolution, and nuclear warfare illumined by man as God's image, Christ as man's liberator, the Church as sign of the world's unity, and the Kingdom as God's reign among men.

We seek thereby to demonstrate the truth of Luther's words, "Not reading and speculation, but living, dying, and being condemned makes a real theologian."

In this volume a biologist and a theologian have teamed together to develop the scientific and religious dimensions of the ecological crisis. In the first half, Paul E. Lutz offers non-scientists an intelligible description of the natural world and some of the basic principles of ecology. The entire earth is depicted as a Spaceship, a finite vehicle on which all living things are intimately dependent upon all the other living and non-living parts of the total environment. The concept of an eco-system is employed to illustrate the delicate interdependence of plants, animals, decomposers, and inanimate substances.

The manifold problems of pollution and population are then explored. Both air and water pollution are described in detail, with special emphasis given to their effects on human health and welfare. The acute pollution problems of solid wastes, excessive noise, and radiation are also highlighted. Finally, the author analyzes the impending crisis connected with man's unprecedented population explosion. It is shown how the human species has achieved a remarkable growth pattern by means of new medical and public health techniques. Yet it is feared that the eventual natural curb on population growth will turn out to be global famines (and accompanying social and military strife) during the last quarter of this century. In conclusion, therefore, an urgent plea is made for controlling family size as the most immediate and effective policy for at least minimizing the worldwide sufferings inevitably ahead.

Two documented conclusions from Professor Lutz's analysis will strike the sensitive reader with special force. On the one hand, "If there is one concept that unifies the thinking about ecology, it is that of the *interrelatedness of life*." On the other hand, "This country [the United States] has about 6% of the world's population and consumes roughly 50% of the world's resources." Here modern ecology supports biblical theology. From a Christian perspective, the ecological catastrophe centers on man: his creaturely need for communal responsibility and his sinful greed in plundering God's good earth.

What is man?[1] As *Homo sapiens* he experiences the ecological crisis with all the rest of Spaceship Earth; but as *imago Dei* he alone knows it, writes books and laws about it, and is able to pray for as well as prey on his fellow creatures. Because it shares in the turmoil of our age, the Church can speak to man's anguished cry, "Who am I?" and "Why am I here?" It can strengthen us in tackling the problems we have (as creatures) by offering us Christ's answer to the problems we are (as sinners). For we find nothing harder than facing ourselves—especially in the presence of the living God. Because this is so, the message of the Bible wants to get us to see ourselves as we really are before God.

The Bible declares that we are all created in the image of God. In and through Adam that image has been corrupted; in and through Christ that same image is being re-created. Thus no man can truly know himself until he first comes to know the God whose holy and loving nature he is to reflect. That is why Jesus Christ, "the image of the invisible God," is so significant for human life (Col. 1: 15). As Savior, he shows us first what God is like; as the Second Adam, he shows us what we can be like. Only through the "mind of Christ" can we hope to regain our true ecological identity as God's earthly managers.

Coming forth from the hand of his Creator, man is to conform to the divine pattern for relational and responsible personhood. "So God created man in his own image . . . male and female he created them . . . And God said to them, 'Be fruitful and multiply, and fill the earth and subdue it; and have dominion over the fish of the sea and over the birds of the air and over every living thing that moves upon the earth'" (Gen. 1: 27-28). In other words, man is to live a full life as a faithful child of God, a loving fellow man,

1. For a fuller description, see my *Man: In Whose Image* (Philadelphia: Fortress, 1961).

and a responsible steward of creation. Liberated by Christ from the forces of evil, Christians "find themselves by losing themselves" in an interrelated life of worship, fellowship, and stewardship.[2]

What does the "mind of Christ" mean for us today? The ecological crisis adds up to the idolatrous worship of the material goods of our labors that Jesus called "mammon." Men created to love God and use things choose rather to love things and try to use God to get those things. Preoccupation with the endless accumulation of things can easily become a matter of ultimate concern. Jesus warns, "You cannot serve both God and mammon" (Matt. 6: 24). When mammon-serving Americans will leave only 50% of the world's resources to the other 94% of God's children struggling to survive on Spaceship Earth, the ecological challenge demands a theological response.

Co-author H. Paul Santmire devotes the second half of the volume to an impassioned plea for a reorientation in human values at this critical juncture in man's ecological life. The issue, he contends, is not the beautification of America, but the survival of humanity. The final four chapters, intended as a personal discourse in practical theology, invite the reader to share the proffered vision of wholeness and renewal for all things.

Thinking ecologically, rather than merely thinking about ecology, calls for a restructuring of our entire way of life. The model of Spaceship Earth is further developed to dramatize the dynamic equilibrium that is ecologically mandatory

2. Those who blame the Bible for sanctioning man's wanton exploitation of the planet in the name of his God-given "dominion" are misreading Genesis through the polluted spectacles of Western economic history. See Ian L. McHarg, *Design with Nature* (Garden City: The Natural History Press, 1969) and Lynn White Jr., "The Historical Roots of our Ecologic Crisis," *Science* 155 (1967). The exegetical evidence for a Christ-centered interpretation of the image of God in terms of human responsibility is reviewed in C. F. D. Moule, *Man and Nature in the New Testament* (Philadelphia: Fortress Facet Books, 1967).

for human survival with justice and freedom. Immediate remedies include the stabilization and reduction of population growth, a radical cut-back in the non-essentials of economic growth, massive programs for recycling and pollution control, the substitution of cooperation for competition as the prevailing ethos of community life, and a thoroughgoing redistribution of wealth.

Beyond these structural reforms, Chaplain Santmire calls for the acceptance of a universal good to serve as the valuational fuel for the moral inhabitants of Spaceship Earth. Life is most beneficially energized by the universal value of love as synthesized in its various aspects: love as *eros* (bodily love in Norman O. Brown), love as *philia* (struggle for social justice in James H. Cone), and love as *agape* (cosmic reconciliation in Teilhard de Chardin). Men will gain a new vision of ecological life in love by combining the divergent trends of thought in religious naturalism, black theology, and catholic ecumenism.

It is suggested that these three forms of love correspond to a universal process of divine creativity that envelops and permeates Spaceship Earth. *Eros, philia,* and *agape* are professed to be rooted in the immediate presence of the God who is living, holy, and gracious. In turn, this triadic congruity determines the shape of an ecstatic lifestyle that interrelates the major dimensions of the human life cycle: the joys of childhood, the protests of adolescence, and the service of adulthood.

Such an ecstatic lifestyle can be developed and deepened among persons willing to covenant with each other to form a global community of mutual support. The Christian Church provides fertile soil for such a venture through a threefold ministry that is priestly, prophetic, and pastoral in witness to Jesus Christ who is at once life-giver, just judge, and self-giving reconciler. In short, the Christian Church at best provides a holistic vision of life's renewal through liturgical celebrations that embody an ecstatic lifestyle during man's pilgrimage through Infinity.

The editor's responsibility to initiate dialogue in confrontation compels me to raise a basic question about Dr. Santmire's provocative essay. It concerns not the wisdom of the ecological conclusions, but the validity of the biblical and theological foundations. The author freely acknowledges that his position differs markedly from "what most major modern Western theologians have maintained" in their common affirmation that "the universe is solely a platform brought into being for the sake of God's history with men." Without quibbling about the adequacy of that particular formulation, there certainly is a key issue at stake here: the proper relation between man and nature under God.

To employ the convenient typology recently suggested by Frederick Elder, there has generally been a radical cleavage between the ecological approaches of 1) the *"exclusionists"* who emphasize the uniqueness of man-in-history distinct from his environment, and 2) the *"inclusionists"* who stress the solidarity of man-in-nature as an integral part of the organic web of life.[3]

Although most classical and modern Christian theologians have affirmed man's biological creatureliness, they have nevertheless also accentuated the Bible's central testimony to God's mighty acts in history through Israel and in Jesus Christ for the redemption of a sinful mankind. On the other hand, many evolutionists and ecologists, unable to verify man's transcendent relation to God—though clearly documenting his avarice toward nature—have generally supported some form of evolutionary naturalism, if anything, as valuational fuel for a finite Spaceship Earth.

Now the problem: can Christians somehow combine the theological particularity of the *"exclusionists"* with the eco-

3. See Frederick Elder, *Crisis in Eden: A Religious Study of Man and Environment* (New York: Abingdon, 1970).

logical universality of the *"inclusionists?"* The author makes an admirable attempt, most impressively in forging some indispensable ethical links between the presently alienated groups of white ecology advocates and black poverty victims in American society. Nevertheless, does the entire venture not betray the construction of an eclectic synthesis that results theologically in the author's feared "unstable compound"? Does not Christian particularity capitulate to a scientific universal*ism* when *eros, philia,* and *agape* are said to differ merely as forms rather than as kinds of love?[4]

Does that not relativize the unique kind of self-giving love divinely revealed on the cross of Christ in contradiction to the scandalous gospel of the New Testament? On so shaky a foundation, what is the inner dynamic beyond formal symmetry that unifies the alleged triadic correspondences with the nature of God, the life cycle of man, the mission of Christ, and the ministry of the Church?

An alternate theological approach, based on a more radical view of man's sin and God's grace, would suggest a consistently sharper distinction (without actual separation!) between the creative and redemptive activity of God. Such a Trinitarian orientation is deemed necessary because only one part of God's creation—man—is created in God's image, falls into sin, and needs redemption. Since nature does not fall into sin, why should Christians try to base the ethical case for ecological renewal on God's redemptive activity through a cosmic Christology? Is the care of the earth not rather the rational responsibility of all men of good will, whatever their faith, whose living God is continually creating his good earth anew both through and among them?

There is no biblical evidence for either a cosmic fall in

---

4. See "Agape" in Gerhard Kittel (ed.), *Theological Dictionary of the New Testament,* Vol. 1 (Grand Rapids, Michigan: Eerdmans, 1964); also Anders Nygren, *Agape and Eros: A Study of the Christian Idea of Love* (London: Society for Promoting Christian Knowledge, 1953).

Adam or a cosmic redemption in Jesus Christ. Nature exists as part of God's creation, under man's suzerainty, but not fallen in sin. For Paul, nature "groans in travail" solely because of its dependence on fallen man and his irresponsible stewardship. It is therefore the prevailing verdict of current New Testament scholarship that, ". . . on a Christian showing, non-human nature has no independent rights."[5]

The destiny of nature is portrayed in the New Testament as a direct by-product of the destiny of man. To cite Paul's metonymic words (Rom. 8: 12), nature has only a man-conditioned hope ("For the creation waits with eager longing for the revealing of the sons of God") as the remedy for its man-conditioned plight (". . . creation was subjected to futility, not of its own will"). In short, ecological renewal does not bring in God's Kingdom, but God's Kingdom does bring in ecological renewal.

Once again, however, our ongoing dialogue on the biblical and theological "why" dare not vitiate the urgency of the author's ethical "what" in regard to ecological renewal. Ours is a pluralistic society with a wide variety of faith and non-

5. See C. F. D. Moule, *op. cit.*, p. 12. This view is challenged as a one-sided and inadequate representation of New Testament thinking in Paul Santmire's earlier study, *Brother Earth: Nature, God, and Ecology in Time of Crisis* (New York: Nelson, 1970). At issue here is the technical problem of how much the New Testament talks about "nature" and the cosmos and with what understanding of them. Specifically involved is the question of how references to "all things" and to *ktisis* are to be taken, in key passages as Col. 1: 15–20 (on which, cf. John Reumann, "The 'Christ Hymn' of Colossians I," in Ivar Asheim, ed., *Christ and Humanity* [Philadelphia: Fortress, 1970], pp. 96–109). The Greek word *ktisis* can refer to (a) God's *act* of creation (Romans 1: 20) or (b) the *result* of creation, "what is created," in the sense of either (1) *creature* (man) (Col. 1: 23), or (2) *creation*. It is in pinning down the precise nuance of this latter sense that controversy centers. *Ktisis* in the sense of "creation" can mean either the human race, all mankind (Mark 16: 15) or the whole created order, including inanimate "nature" (Rom. 1: 25). What, then, is the proper meaning of "new creation" (*kaine ktisis*): is it limited to the Christian believer in his new existence (2 Cor. 5: 17, RSV, "if any one is in Christ, he is a new creature") or does it also imply cosmic renewal (redemption!) of the whole created order?

faith commitments. In no case should our discussions be permitted to provide false comfort to a common enemy: the private and corporate mammon-servers who are now flourishing in filth among us.

In this regard, James T. Megivern recalls that the original sin of Adam is described biblically in terms of man's misuse of the earth's fruit. Then this prototype of sin is repeated by Cain, who despoils the earth with the blood of his brother Abel. Here is the trenchant conclusion, "This is a parable for all times, as biting in its irony as it is perceptive of the human condition: when man destroys his brother, he pollutes the earth; when he pollutes the earth, he destroys his brother . . . and himself."[6]

Similarly poignant, especially for her parents, was the poetic testimony of a sensitive eleven-year old girl entitled "It's Gone":

I walked to the sea, there was nothing there;
Nothing worth seeing, only a scare.

I looked at the sky, there was nothing there;
Nothing worth seeing, just polluted air.

I stared at the ground, there was nothing there;
Nothing worth seeing, yet earth had been rare.

I cried for the world, there was nothing there;
Nothing worth seeing, for too few care.

Philadelphia, Pennsylvania   WILLIAM H. LAZARETH
All Saints' Day, 1971

6. See James T. Megivern, "God's Good Earth and Ours," (New York: The Christophers, n.d.), and also his "Ecology and the Bible," *The Ecumenist,* Vol. 8, No. 5, 1970.

AN INTERDEPENDENT
WORLD

Paul E. Lutz

Preface

On Monday, April 13, 1970, North Americans everywhere were enjoying a routine, carefree evening. Everyone was in high spirits; it had been an exhilarating spring day. The warm temperatures over much of the United States coincided with the appearance of many spring flowers. Aboard Apollo 13, America's third venture in putting men on the surface of the moon, life was also relatively routine. The three astronauts—James A. Lovell, Jr., Fred W. Haise, Jr., and John L. Swigert, Jr.—were already more than 205,000 miles from earth. It was almost 56 hours since liftoff on April 11, and so far life aboard the Apollo 13 complex was "nominal."

At 10:08 p.m. EST, however, Mission Control in Houston received a terse communication from Jack Swigert: "Hey! We've got a problem here!" Within minutes, it became clear both to the Apollo 13 crew and to those on duty at Mission Control that the problem was serious. An oxygen tank in a fuel cell deep within the service module had exploded and in doing so played havoc with many on-board systems. The crucially important environmental systems that supplied the cabin with oxygen, electricity, and other consumables were severely crippled.

These men faced the prospect of death as no others had ever faced it—alone in the bleak, black vastness of space hundreds of thousands of miles from any form of human assistance. Clearly, it would take a major technological achievement to bring them back safely.

The world awoke on April 14 to learn that Lovell, Haise, and Swigert were still in deep trouble. *Odyssey,* their command module, and its lunar module, *Aquarius,* were together hurtling away from the friendly confines of earth toward the moon. Many earthlings were confused to learn that the quickest and most expeditious way back to earth for Apollo 13 was to continue on course and to loop around the moon. This was possible because of the gravitational fields of both the moon and earth and the momentum of the spacecraft. The astronauts, meanwhile, continued trying to make their spacecraft's environment more suitable for human habitation for the three-and-a-half day trip home.

Americans everywhere were deeply concerned over the well-being and safety of their brave comrades a quarter of a million miles away. Many remained close to their radios or television sets to follow the progress of Apollo 13. Millions prayed for the safe return of these three. In an impressive demonstration of corporate concern, thousands of churches held services for the three men.

Earthlings were given hourly reports on the amounts of consumables on board. We were aware that their electricity, food, oxygen, and other life-support elements were present in only limited quantities. The astronauts could not survive there indefinitely. Only by carefully conserving their resources could they hope to return to earth alive.

On April 14, *Odyssey* and *Aquarius* were in the vicinity of the moon. While crossing the dark side of the moon, they fired their rockets and altered their pathway in such a manner as to place themselves into a trajectory proper for the homeward trip. As they reappeared from behind the moon and looked toward their destination, what they saw must have seemed awesome. Set in the cold, black, and seemingly endless expanse of space was the planet Earth. In such a fearful and hostile environment, the earth appeared as an oasis amid the incomprehensible extent of outer space. The photographs they took reveal the earth to be a strikingly bright globe with expanses of white clouds covering the brownish-green continents and deep blue oceans. It was a spectacular sight shared by about only a dozen other mortals.

What the Apollo 13 astronauts viewed was, to be sure, something more than just the end of what they hoped would be a safe journey. They saw very clearly that earth was, in fact, a spaceship. Though obviously earth is a much larger craft than *Odyssey* was, the two are remarkably similar in principle and in function. Vast as our planet is, it remains as finite as *Odyssey,* and the principles governing the conservation of resources are the same for both.

The situation itself was really paradoxical. Here we were on earth praying and hoping for the safe return of *Odyssey* with its passengers. And there were the three *Odyssey* astronauts looking at the remainder of humanity aboard our Spaceship Earth. The hopes of all men were that the mission of Apollo 13 might be terminated with the safe return of the astronauts to earth. Fortunately, for Lovell, Haise, and Swigert, and for everyone on this planet, they were returned safely. Splashdown occurred on April 17 in the Pacific Ocean, and the men were picked up by an American ship shortly thereafter. Thousands of prayers of thanksgiving were offered to God for permitting these men to be returned to us safely.

The lives of the 3½ billion astronauts on board Spaceship Earth are just about as much in peril today as were the men aboard Apollo 13 in 1970. However, the pervasive irony of this analogy is that we on board Spaceship Earth have nowhere else to go to reach a higher level of safety, cleanliness, and comfort where there are ample amounts of natural resources. We are on board our finite craft forever. There is no place else to which we can physically travel. We must begin to treat our spaceship within this context.

Mankind is at this point in space and time on our finite spaceship. All occupants are entirely dependent on the proper use and conservation of everything on board. Proper and moderate use of our mineral resources is necessary. Maintaining the correct atmospheric mixture of oxygen, carbon dioxide, and nitrogen is critical. Renewable resources such as minerals, gases, and water must be returned to their cycles in a reusable form. Solid wastes on board the spacecraft must be efficiently disposed of. It is essential that most of the solid wastes be in a form that can be degraded by decomposer organisms so that such materials will not accumulate. On board noises must be minimized to insure the biological and psychological stability of us astronauts. In short, the environment of the spacecraft must be kept orderly, balanced, and efficient.

Finally, there is an optimum number of persons that can be properly and comfortably supported within the confines of the finite spaceship. In fact, potentially, overpopulation is more dangerous than a malfunctioning of one of the life-support systems, since excess passengers demand more of the on-board consumables and further weaken the fragile balance of components all of us need.

The planet Earth is, in every sense, a spacecraft; everything possible must be done to insure the maintenance of its environment. The following pages deal with the intricate workings of our craft and the ecological checks and balances that are in effect. We can restore the craft's environment only if we fully understand not only its processes, causes, and effects, but also all the ramifications of our attempts at restoration. It is absolutely essential that one understand the physical inner-workings of the entire system.

In addition to a better understanding of the physical aspects of our craft and how all systems function, some basic ethical decisions must be made. To varying degrees each person will be called upon to evaluate the inevitable apparent and possible weaknesses that appear in the craft. The continued success of our trip will depend upon the correct formulation of value judgments and upon crucially important moral and ethical decisions. Interpretive evaluations must be made as "read-outs" are obtained from all the dials indicating the status of the craft. The credibility of signals that run counter to one's "feel of things" must be questioned and appropriate responses initiated.

The main emphasis of the remainder of this book will be to help everyone become better inhabitants of our spaceship. The "hardware" of ecology (the environment, cycles, energy flow, pollution, and considerations of the population explosion) will be treated first. Then will follow a discourse on the "software" (theological interpretations of ethical decisions about the responsible behavior of us astronauts). The survival of space travellers depends upon both the hardware and the software. It is hoped that this volume and others will be of assistance as we continue our trip through space and time, and let us remember that a long trip is better than a short one.

My personal view is that the current environmental crisis can ultimately be alleviated only by a massive shift in our individual and corporate lifestyles. To be sure, science and technology will be able to solve many of our current crises, but they can not provide a panacea for all of our environmental problems. Drastic changes in our economic, sociological, political, moral, ecological, and religious practices and beliefs must occur in order to equip us better to live in relative harmony with nature. Each of us must begin to change our style of living from whatever it might now be to that of a spaceman. This is what ecological renewal is all about: being, acting, thinking, living, and responding like an astronaut on board Spaceship Earth.

Many persons have contributed directly and indirectly to my thinking of the environmental crisis and to potential avenues of restoration. The efforts of my parents, pastors, university colleagues, family, and friends are all deeply appreciated. Special thanks are extended to Besi Morgan, who made many constructive suggestions in the manuscript, and to my wife, Alice, to whom I owe so much, and who typed the entire manuscript. Finally, I would like to dedicate this to my daughter, Carol, in the hope that she and her generation will be better space travellers on Spaceship Earth than were her predecessors.

P. E. L.

Chapter One

Principles of
Ecology

Only during the last five years has society become aware of and concerned about ecology. The word "ecology" is now a part of almost everyone's vocabulary. Yet scarcely a decade ago, it was known almost exclusively to biologists, demographers, some sociologists, and crossword puzzle fans. The laity (non-ecologists) was simply unaware of the growth of that branch of science that deals with environment.

The history of ecology, however, goes back farther than a decade or even a century. As our primate ancestors evolved into modern man some two million years ago, they slowly developed an awareness of their surroundings. Early man utilized environmental information in hunting and trapping animals, finding edible roots, nuts, berries, and other vegetation, and in finding shelter. Natural selection obviously favored those individuals or groups that made the best use of environmental information: those that were either ignorant of or unconcerned about their environment simply did not survive.

Early agrarian societies, which began to develop about 10,000 years ago, were highly dependent upon environmental information. Times of planting and harvesting, methods of fertilizing, crop rotation, erosion control, recognition of fertile and arid soils, and cultivation practices were very much environmental concerns. As knowledge increased about the importance of environmental conditions, there developed many religious rituals. Both superstitious and sound practices regarding crop pests, habits of crop plants, rain dances, worship of weather and fertility gods, and many other activities followed.

The writings of the early Greek philosopher-theologian-scientists clearly reflected environmental concerns. Hippocrates, Theophrastus, and Aristotle were some of the most notable of the nature writers. But during the subsequent eighteen to twenty centuries, environmental understanding progressed very little. Toward the close of this period, there was a reawakening of interest in natural events and processes. French, German, and British naturalists began journeying all over the world investigating the geology, climate, flora, and fauna of distant lands. In 1868, Reiter introduced the term *oekologie,* a word derived from the Greek words *oikos* (=home) and *logos* (=a discussion or study). The term was shortly anglicized to *ecology.* Nevertheless, even though the word "ecology" is about a hundred years old, the formal development of the science itself as a separate branch of biology did not begin until as late as the early twentieth century. Great advances in ecology—indeed, torrents of ecological knowledge—have been developed over the last fifty years by ecologists in America, Europe, Australia, and elsewhere.

To the general public, ecology seems a "young" science, and in terms of formal development it is "young" when compared to such other subdivisions of biology as anatomy and physiology. In a real sense, however, it is the oldest of all sciences, since man has always depended for his survival upon his environment.

Ecology deals, as Odum states, with "the relation of organisms or groups of organisms to their environment."[1]

1. Eugene P. Odum, *Fundamentals of Ecology* (2nd ed.; Philadelphia: W. B. Saunders Company, 1959), p. 4.

Other definitions include the study of the structure and function of nature, and the study of the living environment. All definitions of ecology concern living organisms and their relationship to each other and to their environment. Any factor—including another organism—that directly or indirectly influences an organism is a part of that organism's ecology. Take the ecology of man, for example. Some non-living factors relative to his ecology are ambient temperature, rainfall, the types of soil in which he raises plants, relative humidity, amounts of sunlight, relative purity of his air and water and soil, and countless other features. His living environment includes other persons, animals, plants, and all the numerous influences these have on him. The ecology of man, in short, includes a wide spectrum of factors.

Of necessity, ecology is an interdisciplinary science. The relationship between an organism and its environment is staggeringly complex, and ecologists must be concerned not only with the biology of an organism, but also with its chemistry, physics, behavior, and so on. Despite the apparent confusion, however, there is a considerable degree of order underlying every organism's ecology. The remainder of this chapter will be devoted to a discussion of those principles that are basic to the ecology of all organisms.

ECOSYSTEMS

The term *ecosystem* refers to the interactions of organisms living in a certain area with their non-living environmental factors. The non-living factors, substances, and gradients are termed *abiotic* (= without life) factors. These include gases, salts, water, moisture, currents, wind, temperature, sunlight, and a thousand other inanimate physicochemical events. The living aspects of an ecosystem are termed the *biotic* (= living) components and include all living things in this system, among them plants, animals, and microbes and the many ways in which these interact with each other. Competition, predation, parasitism, decomposition, respiration, photosynthesis and other symbiotic interactions are some of the more familiar biotic processes.

Ecosystems are real entities, not theoretical or conceptual models. Field, forest, and stream—each and all are actual, functioning ecosystems. Though they differ in character, composition, and relative degree of complexity, they share certain functional and structural parameters, several of which will be examined in subsequent pages. Ecosystems are the basic units of ecological study because it is within such systems that organisms interact with their environment. Attention will be given here not only to the structure of ecosystems, but also to the manner in which they function. Both structure and function are intimately related to each other; any treatment of them must necessarily consider them concurrently.

It is by means of energy that organisms perform their many activities. Consequently, any consideration of ecosystems must be concerned with energy. Both the method by which organisms utilize energy and the immediate source of that energy impose a definite pattern of structural and functional organization. Accordingly, we can divide organisms into three types on the basis of their sources of energy:

1) *Producers*—The ultimate source of energy for any ecosystem is sunlight. Producers are those organisms, such as green plants and certain bacteria, that convert sunlight into chemical energy. Such organisms are said to be *autotrophic* (self-feeding), and the process by which this autotrophism takes place is called *photosynthesis*. Photosynthesis is one of the most important biological processes, for it accounts for almost the total conversion of abiotic energy into biotic chemical compounds.

2) *Consumers*—These are organisms that do not produce their own food; instead, they obtain their food from other organisms, usually by eating them. Consumers, most of which are animals, are called *heterotrophic* (=other-feeding).

11

Ecologists recognize several different types of consumers based on the types of food they ingest or consume. Some consumers feed on plants or plant materials. These are called *herbivores* or primary consumers. Other animals feed on the herbivores; these are called *carnivores* or secondary consumers. Carnivores can, in turn, be eaten by other animals called tertiary consumers. There is a transferral of food energy from producers to herbivores to carnivores giving rise to what ecologists call a food chain. This concept will be considered later.

3) A third group of organisms in any ecosystem is the *decomposers*. Decomposers are organisms of decay and are chiefly bacteria and fungi. Decomposers are also heterotrophic organisms, but they do not consume food as animals ingest their food. Rather, decomposers absorb their food after it has been broken down outside their bodies by the activity of their digestive enzymes.

Decomposer populations of any ecosystem are enormous. Their function within an ecosystem is twofold. First, they break down organic remains of producers or consumers that have lived at one time in that area—hence, their name. This prevents the remains of organisms from accumulating. Secondly, as a result of this decomposing process, the chemical elements of which organisms are composed are returned to the abiotic environment, where they become available for reuse. This process is known as *mineralization*.

The fourth component of any ecosystem is the sum of all the *abiotic factors* operative therein. The diversity of these factors has been mentioned earlier. Figure 1 shows the interactions of the four ecosystem components. Solar radiation, incidentally, has a direct effect on all four components, since it supplies heat to the whole environment and is a primary source of energy to certain of the organisms within that environment.

Let us consider a pond, a familiar enough example of an

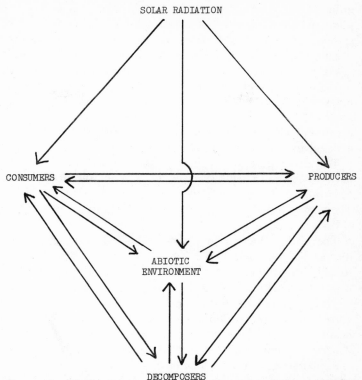

FIGURE 1. *The basic components of an ecosystem showing directions of interactions.*

ecosystem. Everyone has visited a pond and knows about the diversity of life there. Producers in a pond are usually of two main types. One type includes the large rooted or floating plants growing in relatively shallow water and near the shore—cattails, water lilies, and so on. In addition to these large plants, there are the *phytoplankton* (= minute floating plants), most of which are algae. They are quite small (most are microscopic) and very numerous (up to 50

13

million per quart of water). Though photosynthesis takes place within both types of producers as long as the sun is shining, the phytoplankton, because of their vastly greater number, are the more functionally important.

Pond herbivores include those animals that dine off plants —snails, clams, certain fishes, *zooplankton*, (=minute floating animals), and certain insect larvae. Carnivores include other fishes, insects, frogs, and worms. Examples of tertiary consumers are turtles, otters, and other animals like raccoons and hawks that might occasionally visit the pond.

The decomposers (the bacteria and fungi) have already been discussed. They are exceedingly numerous in a pond, especially at the bottom, to which organisms sink after death. There may be as many as 30 million bacteria in one ounce of bottom mud.

The abiotic factors in the pond include the water and its various parameters (i.e., the amount and types of dissolved gases, minerals, and nutrients), the temperature of the water, the length of the daylight hours, the angle of the sun, rainfall, the nature of the underlying rocks and soil, and waves and currents. Our pond is not just a point of scenic beauty. It is an ecosystem—a dynamic unit containing within itself an incredible diversity of plants, animals, and microbes —as well as certain inorganic elements, all of which interact. In order to function properly, each organism within and each component of the ecosystem must depend upon every other organism and component.

The idea of interrelatedness is a fundamental precept of ecology. Nevertheless, just as no organism is sufficient unto itself, neither is any ecosystem. Every ecosystem is dependent upon those that are adjacent to it. Our pond, for instance, is dependent upon the springs or streams that flow into it, and these bring to it a host of new and different biotic and abiotic factors. Likewise the forest, field, or pasture that surrounds it adds minerals, nutrients, detritus, and so on.

The concept of interrelatedness can be extended globally to include all ecosystems. The *biosphere* is that portion of the earth in which ecosystems operate and where they illustrate the concept of interdependence. The biosphere extends from the heights of mountains to the depths of the oceans. Living organisms may occur as deep as twenty feet in the soil and miles into the atmosphere. For all practical purposes, however, the biosphere is a thin mantle several thousand feet thick surrounding the entire globe. It is in this thin band that we observe the interrelatedness among organisms, among ecosystem components, and among ecosystems.

It is impossible to overstate the importance of understanding the concept of interrelatedness. Imagine an enormous three-dimensional fish net, each section of which represents a separate organism. What happens to one section, either directly or indirectly, sooner or later influences all the others. The phrase "web of life" is an appropriate metaphor indeed.

One case in point will help illustrate this idea of interrelatedness. During the Pacific campaign of World War II, American soldiers invaded, conquered, and occupied a number of islands that had been controlled previously by the Japanese. Among these was the island of Borneo.

Prior to the war, the people of Borneo had achieved an equilibrium with respect to some organisms living on that island. For several hundred years, their cat population had slowly gained the upper hand over the indigenous rat population and finally had the latter under firm control. So effective was the cat-rat predatory relationship, that the cats had also to be fed by the natives. The usual table scraps helped somewhat, but to supplement their diets further, the cats began feeding on geckos, small lizards common to that area. The main diet of the geckos was a variety of flies also native to the region.

When the Americans came to Borneo, they brought with them a newly-discovered insecticide called DDT. Like most other South Pacific islands, Borneo had plenty of mosquitoes. The newcomers found that they were fierce biters and that they impaired sleep, work, and so on. So they sprayed everything with DDT. It proved to be lethal to about 98% of the island's mosquitoes, so the misery of the American soldier was greatly alleviated. Unfortunately, because of the interrelatedness of organisms and ecosystems, the influences of DDT did not die with the mosquitoes.

The various species of flies in the area were more tolerant of the DDT. They absorbed it into their bodies, like the mosquitoes, but only an insignificant number of them died as a result. Many of the others, their bodies laden with insecticide, were eaten by the geckos. One result of this was that highly concentrated amounts of DDT began to build up in the bodies of the geckos. So great was this concentration that when the geckos in turn were eaten by the cats, practically all of the cats in Borneo died of DDT poisoning. Of course, in the absence of cats, the rat population of Borneo began to explode. Finally, the U.S. Army had to spend hundreds of thousands of dollars importing cats into Borneo to help fight the rat plague. Cats even had to be parachuted into remote villages that were otherwise inaccessible.

This illustrates perfectly the concept of interrelatedness, but to understand that concept fully, certain other ecological concepts must be explored. The first of these has to do with mineral cycles.

BIOGEOCHEMICAL CYCLES

"Bio" refers to living organisms and "geo" refers to the soil, air, water, and rocks of the earth. The term "biogeochemical cycle," therefore, refers to the natural passage of chemicals or minerals from living organisms to the abiotic environment and back again to organisms. The chemical components out of which all organisms are constructed never wear out. They are used over and over again. This process of reuse is made possible largely through the activity of decomposers, which has already been described. Moreover, the passage of chemical materials from plants and animals to decomposers to the abiotic environment and back again to plants is definitely cyclical, and this phenomenon forms the basis of another fundamental principle of ecology.

The quantities of minerals in the soil of this planet are the same now as at any point since the beginning of life. We have neither gained nor lost any (except for a few artificially created ones). For example, an atom of iron making up one hemoglobin molecule in each of us has undoubtedly been a part of thousands of diverse organisms in the past, ranging from dinosaurs and seaweed to insects and mastodons. Similarly, a phosphorus atom in one of our brain cells has, at one time or another during the past three billion years, been a part of hundreds of thousands of plants, animals, and decomposers.

Of the ninety-two naturally-occurring elements, between thirty and forty are known to be required by living organisms. Certain elements, such as oxygen, carbon, hydrogen, and nitrogen, are required by organisms in relatively large amounts. Other elements, known as trace elements, are needed only in minute quantities. Regardless of the amounts involved, however, all minerals are subject to biogeochemical cycles. Consider, for example, the cycle undergone by nitrogen, as illustrated in Figure 2.

For the sake of convenience, the illustration omits most of the complexities involved in the nitrogen cycle and shows only principal aspects. The major reservoir of nitrogen is nitrogen gas, which makes up about 79% of our atmosphere. All organisms live amid this nitrogen-rich atmosphere. Still, atmospheric nitrogen is utilized directly by only a very few different organisms. For most, gaseous nitrogen must be con-

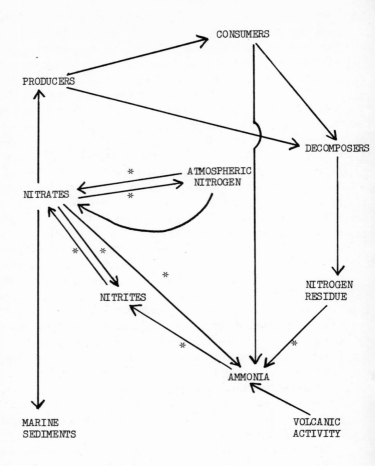

* Bacterial Activity

FIGURE 2. *A diagrammatic representation of the nitrogen cycle.*

verted into a more usable form, nitrate, which is produced by the activity of a number of bacteria and certain algae.

Farmers have known for centuries about the virtues of raising leguminous plants (peas, clover, beans, etc.) intermittently with other crops. Living in association with the roots of these plants are nitrogen-fixing bacteria. They convert large quantities of gaseous nitrogen into the more usable nitrates (up to 500 lbs. of nitrogen per acre per year in clover fields). Lightning striking the earth can also convert nitrogen into nitrates. Other bacteria convert nitrates back into gaseous nitrogen. For green plants, however, nitrates are the most usable form of nitrogen. They are a major component of fertilizer; indeed, as every farmer knows, the price of fertilizer is directly related to the amount of nitrogen it contains.

Plants absorb nitrates through their root system, and the nitrogen is converted into plant protein, a major chemical component of plants. Such plant proteins are converted into animal proteins via food chains. When organisms die their nitrogen-rich proteins are broken down by decomposers into ammonia. Then, by the activity of bacteria, ammonia is converted into nitrites and then into nitrates. Certain bacteria may denitrify the nitrates back to nitrites, ammonia, or to nitrogen. Certain nitrates are temporarily removed from circulation by marine sediments, at the same time that other nitrogen is returned to the cycle via volcanism.

Another mineral cycle will be considered to show how a very important element (phosphorus) also circulates between the biotic and abiotic components of an ecosystem. The phosphorus cycle is shown in Figure 3.

Phosphates in soil or water are absorbed by plants; they may then be passed on to animals via food chains. Eventually, however, organisms die, and during the process of decomposition, bacteria release phosphorus into the soil or water. Some of the phosphates are removed for a time from

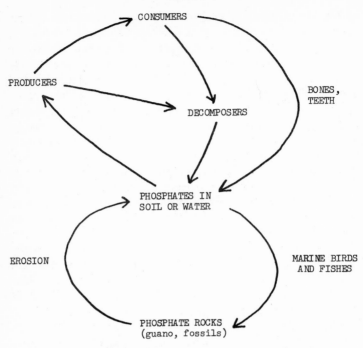

FIGURE 3. *A simplified diagram of the phosphorus cycle.*

circulation as phosphates are converted into rocks. This is accomplished by a precipitation of phosphorus, the tremendous deposits of guano by birds in Peru, and by fossilization of marine organisms. Eventually, some of the phosphorus-rich rocks are exposed to the elements eroding the rocks away, thus returning the phosphates to the cycle. The reservoir for the phosphorus cycle is not in the atmosphere, as is the case with nitrogen, but in rocks and other deposits. The phosphorus cycle is a critical one in that more phosphorus is being removed from circulation via deposits than is being returned to the cycle via erosion. Eventually, man will have to mine phosphorus in order to return it to circulation.

All minerals circulate in basically similar cycles between the living and non-living elements in nature. Unfortunately, other things cycle too, such as DDT and other pesticides, radioactive materials, and mercury, to mention a few.

Many of the activities of man are inadvertently interrupting vital mineral cycles. We create large numbers of things in a non-biodegradable form, and thus tie up minerals indefinitely. We try to eliminate or reduce one type of organism in our midst and thereby short-circuit the cycle. We raise the temperature of the water by hydro-electric generators and thus alter the rate of cycling. Man must now be concerned with the amounts of minerals involved, their arrangement in space, the forms they take, and their rates of flow and change. Any change in an ecosystem, whether in abiotic substances, autotrophs, or heterotrophs, obviously is going to affect the entire ecosystem eventually. Mankind's chief concern in the future should be to minimize such ecological upsets and to maintain the delicate balance of nature.

ENERGETICS

One of the most basic characteristics of any ecosystem is that it is always concerned with *energy*. Every biological reaction occurring within an individual organism and every reaction involving a biotic component within an ecosystem involves energy. In a given organism thousands of energy changes take place every second of every day. The passage of energy within an ecosystem is a major concern. Coupled with mineral cycles, the flow of energy in an ecosystem is *the* most significant principle operative within ecosystems.

For our purposes energy may be defined as the ability to do work. Though several laws of thermodynamics have been developed to describe energetic events, only two are pertinent here. The First Law of Thermodynamics states that energy can be converted from one form into another, but can neither be created nor destroyed. A familiar example of energy conversion is the use of water power to turn turbines, thereby converting water energy into mechanical energy, then electrical energy, which is later converted into light energy. This process, however, does not involve either the creation or the destruction of energy, since solar energy entering our atmosphere is precisely balanced by energy leaving our planet as heat radiation.

The Second Law of Thermodynamics holds that conversions of energy are never 100% efficient. A certain loss of energy, usually in the form of heat, takes place at every conversion. Again, it is not that any energy is destroyed; it is simply that some energy becomes unavailable for reuse. The light energy emitted from electric lamps is less than the energy of the water power. Some of this initial energy was lost as water molecules bumped into each other and as friction developed heat in the turbines; more was lost as a result of electrical resistance in the wiring and of heat from the bulbs. Energy is not being destroyed but is being dispersed (and made more unavailable) as heat. It is because of the Second Law of Thermodynamics that every internal combustion engine must have an exhaust.

In terms of ecology, energy is involved principally in photosynthesis, food transfer, and decay. This introduces the concept of food chains. A *food chain* is the conversion of food energy that begins with plant photosynthesis and that continues when the plants are eaten by herbivores and the herbivores are eaten by carnivores. In natural communities organisms whose food is obtained from plants by the same number of steps are said to belong to the same *trophic* (food) *level*. Thus, green plants occupy the first trophic level (producer level); herbivores, the second level (primary consumer level); carnivores, which eat the herbivores, the third level (secondary consumers), and perhaps a fourth level (tertiary consumers). The decomposers would occupy the last trophic level. An example of a simplified food chain would be:

grass ⟶ rabbit ⟶ fox ⟶ puma
(producer)   (herbivore)   (primary   (secondary
                                carnivore)   carnivore)

It is important to have an understanding of the relationships between trophic levels and energy considerations. Because of the ultimate importance of energy and the laws of thermodynamics that govern it, the energetics of an ecosystem become the primary concern in the stability of the ecosystem.

As an example of ecosystem energy flow, Figure 4 shows energy values in Silver Springs, Florida, at the producer and herbivore levels. Solar radiation is the only energy source available for incorporation into food energy. Less than 50% of solar radiation reaches an ecosystem. Most is reflected back into space or is absorbed by the atmosphere. Of that which reaches the earth's surface, more than 75% does not

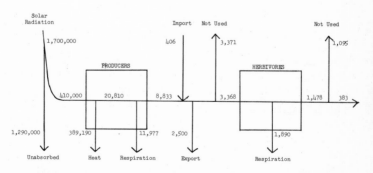

FIGURE 4. *Energy flow in Silver Springs, Florida, at producer and herbivore levels. Data are kilocalories per square meter per year. (After H. P. Odum, "Trophic Structure and Productivity of Silver Springs, Florida,"* ECOLOGICAL MONOGRAPHS 27 *[1957], pp. 55-112.)*

strike any green plants and is therefore not absorbed by them. Moreover, of the 410,000 kilocalories that the plant converts into plant food, almost 60% is used for respiration. Respiration frees chemical food energy and makes some of it available for those functions necessary for the plant's survival (i.e., transport, repair, cell division, maintenance, etc.). Because of the Second Law of Thermodynamics, much of this energy released by respiration is lost as heat. So the net food production by producers is only 8,833 kilocalories—about 0.55% of the solar radiation striking the earth and only slightly more than 2% of the light absorbed. Some of this net energy is exported downstream, and much of it is simply unavailable for the herbivores at the next trophic level, which leaves only a small fraction of the initial energy available and usable by the herbivores.

Figure 4 also illustrates the energy flow at the herbivore level and indicates the energy lost via respiration and made unavailable for the next trophic level. The efficiency of herbivores in this example (comparing the 3,368 kcal. as intake with the 383 kcal. as produced) is only about 10%.

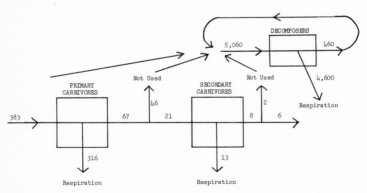

FIGURE 5. *Energy flow in Silver Springs, Florida, at carnivore and decomposer levels. Data are kilocalories per square meter per year. (After H. P. Odum,* ECOLOGICAL MONOGRAPHS *27 [1957], pp. 55-112.)*

Figure 5 shows the dissipation of energy at the primary and secondary carnivore levels as well as the energy loss at the decomposer level. The energy not used by the next trophic levels in the preceding figure is the principal source of energy for the decomposers, which restore to the atmosphere all of the remaining energy in a biologically unusable form—heat. Hence, all of the energy entering this ecosystem has been lost as heat or else been converted into food energy.

Because of the Second Law of Thermodynamics, energy cannot cycle repeatedly, as can minerals; instead, *energy flows*. Energy must constantly be supplied from the sun, and organisms use it rather inefficiently. The inefficiency of organisms and their respiration result in the constant dissipation of energy back out into space in a form unusable by organisms again.

In the energetics of an ecosystem, there are two constants: a constant source of energy and the high but constant degree of inefficiency of organisms. Consequently, only a finite number of organisms (including man) can be maintained at any one level. Organisms at one trophic level can significantly increase their numbers only by occupying a lower trophic level. Asia, for instance, can support its enormous population only because Asians are, for the most part, herbivorous. They cannot afford the luxury of having food energy pass through one or two consumers before they use it. For this reason they do not enjoy much beef, lamb, or fowl in their diets. These basic concepts of energy within organisms and ecosystems have considerable effect on the economic, political, and religious aspects of mankind.

LIMITING FACTORS

It has been known for over a century that agricultural crops thrive only to the extent that all required minerals are present in sufficient amounts. If one essential element is present only in minimal amounts, and even if all other minerals are abundantly available, the plants grown in that soil will be severely limited. It follows that no organism or group of organisms is any stronger than its weakest ecological link. This concept is known as the Law of the Minimum.

Shortly after the turn of the century, ecologists began to realize that an overabundance of ecological requirements might also inhibit the well-being of organisms. Too much, as well as too little, of any environmental component would be intolerable to organisms. Subsequently, tolerance limits were found to be quite important to all organisms. Figure 6 shows a continuum of organismic responses to a given environmental condition. Indicated are the zones of intolerance, the stress zones, and the area where the condition is optimum.

A *limiting factor* is any condition that approaches or exceeds the tolerance limits (either maximum or minimum) of an organism. Concurrent tolerance limits for a given organism may be very narrow for one condition and very wide for another. In addition, different seasons or life-history stages may alter the tolerance limits for a given condition.

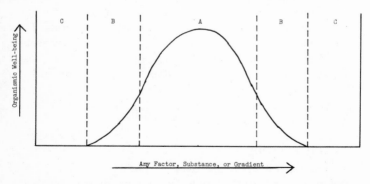

FIGURE 6. *The tolerance range by an organism to a given environmental condition. (A = optimal zone; B = zones of stress conditions; C = zones of intolerance.)*

Any abiotic factor can function as a limiting factor. Familiar factors limiting the activities of organisms include temperature, water, light, relative humidity, oxygen, carbon dioxide, minerals, and soil composition. Some biotic factors, such as density, parasitism, competition, and population size, may also function as limiting factors.

Limiting factors play an important role in the well-being of both organisms and ecosystems. Too much of some factor results in stress or the death of organisms. Certain of the pollutants now threatening our environmental integrity are present in amounts approaching the point of intolerance to many organisms. Conversely, some of our current ecological problems concern substances that are present in increasingly diminishing amounts due to acyclical biogeochemical cycles. Copper and phosphorus, for example, are reasonably scarce and may soon become limiting factors for organisms.

EQUILIBRIUM

Ecosystems possess a high degree of stability if allowed to continue undisturbed. This stability is one of the most important inherent properties of ecosystems. There are many checks and balances to help dampen out oscillations that appear in the various populations or processes that are components of an ecosystem. These forces and counterforces are considered to be *homeostatic mechanisms* that are highly instrumental in effecting ecosystem stability. All naturally occurring ecosystems have these compensatory or regulatory forces that assist in maintaining the *status quo*. Such mechanisms are found at all levels of biological organization from cell to organism to ecosystem. At the ecosystem level these mechanisms make possible a fairly constant set of conditions, rates, and processes within a given system.

In many, and perhaps all, ecosystems the degree of equilibrium is directly related to the diversity of organisms comprising the ecosystem. Indeed, the most stable ecosystems are those in which the diversity of various organisms is greatest. All ecosystems age or mature, and this process of maturation is described as an evolution toward greater diversity.[2] With greater diversity there is less likelihood that a major shift in any ecosystem component would adversely affect the system as a whole. Examples of a diverse, stable ecosystem are an oak-hickory forest, a beech-maple forest, an estuary, a maple-basswood forest, and a river.

Conversely, the least stable ecosystem is one in which there is present the minimum of diversity of fauna and flora. A homogeneous, unstable system has only a temporary existence both spatially and temporally. All ecosystems that man has tampered with are unstable, and the degree of their instability is directly related to the degree of man's intervention. Examples of unstable ecosystems are farm ponds and other impoundments, fields, lawns, parks, pastures, etc. Such systems, if allowed to exist for even a year without man's influence, undergo dramatic and significant changes in their nature and composition.

Consider a cultivated field of corn, for example. Initially, a virgin, stable, and highly diversified hardwood forest probably had to be removed in order for this land to be farmed. At present this ecosystem is composed of only one kind of organism—corn. To insure its high productivity, the farmer probably sprays it repeatedly with various pesticides. This farmer is engaged in *monoculture,* the cultivation of only one type of plant per area. The mere absence of diversity makes monoculture an unstable arrangement because, in spite of the attention the agriculturist gives his corn field, he can never be sure that some new pest, or blight, or something else will not come along and decimate his crop.

Ecologists and many agricultural experts are now advocating *polyculture,* the growing of a larger number of different

2. Edward J. Kormondy, *Concepts of Ecology* (Englewood Cliffs, New Jersey: Prentice-Hall, 1969), p. 159.

plants in the same field. This can be accomplished by strip farming, for example, in which several rows of a given crop are interspersed with rows of other crops. This, of course, adds to the diversity and enhances the stability of the area. More opportunities would exist for natural checks and balances to operate against invasions of diseases, parasites, and the like. The farmer could then use lesser amounts of ecologically-detrimental herbicides and pesticides. The area would experience a lessening of land erosion and water pollution. Greater levels of energy utilization and higher rates of biogeochemical cycling could also be realized. All these factors are a part of increased diversity and enhance ecosystem stability. As Odum has stated, *"Conservation of the ecosystem* rather than *conservation of this or that species . . .* would seem to be the most sensible approach."[3] It is obviously in our best interests to preserve and enhance the diversity of life that is the product of millions of years of evolution. Odum continues, "The diversity of life should be looked upon as a national and international treasury."[4]

Following this brief exploration of some of the more important ecological principles and processes, the consequences of environmental pollution and overpopulation can now be viewed with greater meaning. Air pollution, which would reduce solar radiation, pollution that might eliminate herbivores, and oil pollution, which decimates the producer ranks: all have dire consequences for man. All organisms are inexorably woven into the fabric of the ecosystem, and they are utterly dependent upon the cycling of minerals and the orderly flow of energy. Various substances and requirements must be supplied in amounts approaching optimum. Of utmost importance is that ecosystems remain stable or in a state of relative equilibrium. Any break or fracture in the

3. Eugene P. Odum, *Ecology* (New York: Holt, Rinehart and Winston, 1963), p. 35.
4. *Ibid.*

"chain of life" eventually affects all organisms. Man is an integral part of nature and highly dependent upon a homeostatic environment, that is, one with relatively constant conditions.

If there is one concept that unifies the thinking about ecology, it is that of the *interrelatedness of life*. Hopefully, there will be generations in the future who can talk about life's interrelatedness.

Chapter Two

Pollution

One of the most insidious ways in which man is disrupting his environment is by polluting it. Pollutants are impurities that occur in a myriad of forms in air, water, food, soil, and elsewhere. Some pollution of air and water occurs naturally and has since the beginning of time. Indeed, a pollution-free atmosphere would make a colorful sunrise or sunset impossible. Pure water would not have the beautiful hues of blues and greens so characteristic of "unpolluted" water. Every body of water and every volume of air normally contains some pollution in the form of chemicals, dust, gases, and particles of various sorts. This "background" pollution is a natural phenomenon and is usually of such low magnitude as to be only incidental to man.

What follows will be a consideration of the ways in which man has added immeasurably to the environmental pollution levels. Environmental quality has deteriorated rapidly in recent years due to the addition of a number of man-made or man-induced biologically active substances that are termed "pollutants." Overpopulation, industrialization, and modern technology are the principal sources of innumerable new and exotic substances that threaten the continued existence of many forms of life, including man. But just as important as the direct influences that pollution has on man is what the effects of man's activities will have on the ecosystems of the earth. Environmental processes, such as biogeochemical cycles and energy flow, are quite sensitive to environmental pollution. Pollution is a complex phenomenon and one that has profoundly important ramifications for environmental quality. And though the forms of pollution that do not directly concern *Homo sapiens* are important, for purposes of this book, considerations will be restricted to those pollutants produced by man and that, in turn, influence the human species.

AIR POLLUTION

Air pollution is a familiar environmental problem to most inhabitants of industrialized countries. Every major metropolitan area on this planet has air pollution problems. The influences of industrialization and urbanization upon air quality in even the most remote rural areas are evidenced by smarting eyes and the increasingly visible atmospheric brown or blue palls. The global wind currents insure that no person can be insulated from air pollution for very long. Radioactive materials, for example, produced by atmospheric nuclear explosions in Asia appear over North America about a week after their creation. Thus, air pollutants cannot be restricted to the areas in which they are produced; rather, they are distributed in areas far from their source.

Atmospheric pollutants are of diverse character and origin. Some of the more common air pollutants are particulate matter (dust particles); gases, such as carbon monoxide and oxides of sulfur and nitrogen; and hydrocarbons (a variety of substances composed of the elements hydrogen and carbon). Many of the substances emitted into the air are relatively harmless. But the energy from the sun can cause a multitude of photochemical reactions to occur. Thus, a relatively innocuous chemical can be converted by sunshine into a much more potent pollutant.

Sources of air pollution are equally as diverse as the pollutants themselves. The major sources include the burning of fossil fuels (coal, gas, oil) for interior heating and cooling, internal combustion engines (cars, buses, trucks, etc.), the burning of a variety of things (garbage, charcoal, forest fires, etc.), cigarette smoke, and a large number of paper and steel mills, factories, power stations, refineries, chemical plants, and industrial firms.

In the U.S. alone, the annual output of air pollutants is staggering. Automobiles annually emit 66 million tons of carbon monoxide, 7 million tons of oxides of sulfur and nitrogen, and 1 million tons of particulate materials. About 4 million tons of sulfur dioxide are emitted via chimneys in our country each year. An estimated total in excess of 160 million tons of gases, particles, poisons, and filth are produced annually as air pollutants in this country from all sources. This tonnage is greater than our annual steel production. An additional 16 million tons of air contaminants, such as natural fog and pollen, affect humans to varying degrees each year.

Air pollutants cause a number of human concerns. First, much of the particulate matter affects persons as dirt, and cleaning bills are accordingly higher for clothes, household appointments, building exteriors and interiors, etc. Many air pollutants cause rubber to crack, paint to peel, and fabrics to deteriorate. Living things are also affected; certain plants and animals, for example, die. The health of humans is also intimately affected by air pollution. There is a strong correlation between the incidence of air pollutants and lung cancer, emphysema, lung damage, asthma, and other respiratory diseases. Some other less severe human symptoms attributable to air pollution are headaches, loss of coordination, nausea, burning of eyes, coughing, and bronchitis.

Perhaps the oldest form of air pollution is sulfur dioxide. Some of this gas was emitted even when earliest man burned wood, dried dung, or peat. But the introduction of coal for heating and cooking vastly accelerated the emission of sulfur dioxide. When coal burns a number of sulfur-containing compounds, including sulfur dioxide, are released and produce smoke. The combination of smoke and fog, so common around London in the 1800's, prompted an Englishman to coin the word "smog" about the turn of the century.

The air pollutants in smog may be chiefly in the form of sulfur dioxide, smoke, or the result of a photochemical alteration of a wide variety of air pollutants. The smogs of New York or Los Angeles or any of the major metropolitan areas are a clear reminder of air pollution and the havoc it can cause in human populations. In the great London fog of December, 1952, there were 4,000 fatalities attributed to the smog. A similar meteorological event in New York City in 1963 killed more than 400 residents. At Donora, Pennsylvania, in October, 1948, more than 40% of the entire population suffered adverse effects from the smog—as many readers will remember.

Another major source of air pollution (and the resulting smog) is the internal combustion engines of cars, buses, and other gasoline-powered devices. Automobiles cause about 65% of all air pollution. Gasoline is a fuel that does not burn completely to carbon dioxide and water. Rather, a number of intermediate products are formed that become gaseous air pollutants when exhausted. This diversity of hydrocarbons, oxides of nitrogen and carbon and sulfur, and other pollutants can be drastically altered by sunlight to produce photochemical pollutants that potentially are lethal to man, plants, and other animals.

Because of the incomplete combustion of gasoline in an automobile engine, engine knocks develop, and an additive, tetraethyl lead, is used to reduce this undesirable feature. Tetraethyl lead, however, functions like any other metal poison and the right concentration of it is fatal. Since the invention of the automobile in the late 1800's, the lead content of the average American has increased 125-fold to a level approaching the maximum tolerance level. Other gasoline additives include metal deactivators, antirust and anti-icing compounds, lubricants, antioxidants—the list goes on. Such engines produce an almost innumerable variety of pollutants.

Carbon monoxide is another major air pollutant emanating principally from automobiles. It is a potentially lethal gas that irreversibly combines with hemoglobin in the blood. This hemoglobin-carbon monoxide complex blocks the normal process of oxygen combining loosely with hemoglobin in the lungs; thus, persons suffocate as a result of carbon monoxide poisoning. The human body tolerates concentrations of this gas up to 10 parts per million (ppm) without effects. Detrimental effects begin to appear at concentrations of 20-30 ppm. At a busy intersection in a large city one may inhale 20-30 ppm, and a person stopped behind a car at a red light may get a dosage in excess of 350 ppm.[1]

Cigarette smoke is also a major source of air pollutants, especially in enclosed areas. Such smoke contains oxides of sulfur, nitrogen, and carbon as well as the very lethal hydrogen cyanide. Long-term exposures to hydrogen cyanide above 10 ppm are known to be dangerous. Yet the reported concentration of this gas in cigarette smoke is, astonishingly, about 1,600 ppm.[2]

In addition to smog, another visible manifestation of air pollution is termed a temperature inversion. As most persons know, especially any pilot or mountain climber, air temperatures decrease as altitude increases. Air temperatures one mile up are considerably colder than those at ground level. During the autumn and winter months especially, the surface air cools off early in the morning. That stratum of air several thousand feet up remains at the same temperature and may be warmer than surface air. Under these conditions there is

1. Richard H. Wagner, *Environment and Man* (New York: W. W. Norton & Company, 1971), p. 185.
2. Philip H. Abelson, "A Damaging Source of Air Pollution", *Science*, 158 (22 December, 1967), p. 1527.

a temperature increase with increasing height resulting in a condition called an inversion.

An inversion is a layer of warm air sandwiched between two cooler strata of air. All inversions exhibit a damping action of the warm layer over the cooler bottom layer. This is like a lid on a pot and prevents mixing of the air over a city or valley basin. The air pollutants issuing from automobiles, chimneys, and smokestacks are trapped under the inverted warm layer that is acting as a lid. The pollutants cannot penetrate this inversion layer, so they spread out laterally throughout the entire basin. As a result, air pollutants tend sometimes to accumulate to dangerous levels.

Two other factors operative in inversions make them dangerous. First, they occur frequently in autumn and winter when furnaces are operating at maximum, and this adds considerably to the pollution load. Secondly, inversion layers are warm and dry and usually develop in cloudless conditions. Solar energy interacts with the trapped pollutants and causes them to be converted into new photochemical pollutants. The photochemical smogs of Los Angeles are quite different from the smoke smogs of London.

Finally, another effect of air pollution is what is known as the "greenhouse effect." Solar energy enters our atmosphere, for the most part, in short wave lengths (ultraviolet). Much of this energy is absorbed by the earth's surface and is radiated back out into space as heat energy in long wave lengths (infra-red). Carbon dioxide, a rather common atmospheric gas, does not absorb much of the energy of incoming ultraviolet radiation but absorbs to a much greater degree the outgoing infra-red energy. The more carbon dioxide there is in the atmosphere, the more energy will be absorbed, thus raising the temperature of the atmosphere. The same phenomenon happens in a greenhouse or a closed car on a hot day when the heat absorbed greatly outweighs any ability to reflect the heat. During this century, the carbon dioxide content of the atmosphere has risen from 290 to 330 parts per million.[3] This small carbon dioxide content has undoubtedly raised the world's temperature by a small amount. An elevation of carbon dioxide content to 600 ppm would raise the earth's temperature by about 2° F. The polar icecaps would slowly melt, raising the level of the oceans of the world. A continued thermal increase of 10-15° F. would drastically alter all the ecosystems of the world by completely melting the polar icecaps and glaciers. This would raise the ocean levels by an estimated 400 feet, which would flood vast areas of our coastlines.

What are the sources of carbon dioxide? Each person respiring adds a very small amount of this gas to the atmosphere. The respiratory activities of all organisms, both plants and animals, are contributory. But the main source now is the combustion of fossil fuels—coal, natural gas, and petroleum—in furnaces and automobiles, which adds an estimated 0.23 percent per year to the atmospheric content of carbon dioxide.

The greenhouse effect, because of its tendency toward self-perpetuation, may be the ultimate manifestation of the destruction of life on this planet. As the atmospheric temperature rises, because of increased amounts of carbon dioxide, the respiration rate of organisms increases also; this produces carbon dioxide at a faster rate and causes a higher atmospheric temperature. This snowballing effect would be impossible to stop and would spell disaster within a short period of time. Other meteorological events can also be modified by air pollutants. Air pollution can affect light penetration, rainfall, and cloud cover—to mention only a few.

Air pollution should concern everyone because our continued existence depends upon relatively clean air. Each individual should work toward the development and use of

3. Arthur S. Boughey, *Man and the Environment* (New York: Macmillan Company, 1971), p. 324.

various technological devices that are currently being designed to control air pollutants. So many vested interests are involved with the economy and our industrialized society that an enormous amount of inertia must be overcome to make possible the legislation that can enforce pollution laws and restrict the continued practices of air pollution. As Richard Wagner has stated, "The significance of all types of air pollution has begun to dawn upon us and the options are clearly focused, perhaps for the first time in man's history. Continued inaction in dealing with these problems is unconscionable for our generation, and suicidal for the next."[4]

WATER POLLUTION*

One of the commonest chemical compounds in the environment is water. This planet should have been called Ocean, not Earth, since about 73% of the surface of it is covered with water. Approximately 98% of all water is in the oceans and seas. Most of the rest is locked up as ice at the polar regions. Only a very small amount of water is present as fresh water in rivers, lakes, streams, and in the ground. Water is unique; it is the only known liquid substance to occur naturally in the universe.

Biologically, water is a vital compound. Organisms respire, digest, absorb, reproduce, and undertake all physiological activities in an aqueous medium. In living organisms water comprises from 65 to 95% of their weight. Water is another of the "renewable" or cyclic resources, and life is critically dependent upon the cycling of clean water.

4. Wagner, *op. cit.,* p. 195.

* Adapted from articles by Paul E. Lutz, "Our Hostile Environment", *The Alumni News,* University of North Carolina at Greensboro, Summer, 1969, pp. 2–8; and Paul E. Lutz, "Water Pollution: Our Effluence of Affluence," *Proceedings, Third Annual Chancellor's Conference, Man and His Environment,* University of North Carolina at Greensboro, January 6, 1971.

The familiar adage, "Water, water everywhere, and not a drop to drink," generally conjures up a mental picture of a shipwrecked man floating on a raft far at sea and slowly dying of thirst. But it has almost as much relevance to an individual in the 1970's lounging beside the once-beautiful Potomac River or the once-picturesque Lake Erie.

The rivers and streams of America are sick. President Johnson in his State of the Union Message in 1965 reported that every major river system in this country was polluted. This is indeed a tragedy for the richest, most prosperous, most advanced nation in the world. What has happened to turn most of the rivers and waterways in this nation into extensive sewer systems? It seems that prosperity has come at an extremely high price. Twentieth-century affluence has brought twentieth-century effluence. The quality of water appears to decline as economy and technology advance.

Many rivers and lakes are filled with municipal wastes from factories, meat processors, assembly plants, breweries, and from the cities that line their shores. Many Maine rivers are full of tan, foamy pulp from the numerous paper mills. The Delaware River has industrial complexes that run from Trenton, New Jersey, to Wilmington, Delaware. Many beaches in the area have been closed because of pollution and the resulting high bacterial count. Every day, New York City dumps 200 million gallons of waste sewage into the Hudson River.

Lake Erie is almost dead. Only a few species of organisms can exist there now. Beaches are closed to swimming and boating has declined. Tapwater in the area has an unpleasant odor and appearance. Lake Michigan, from which Chicago draws most of its drinking water, and into which steel mills pour metallic acids and oil wastes, is almost as bad. It has acquired the name "Killer Lake" because thousands of water fowl have died mysteriously on its shores.

The Ohio River flows through much of the populated, industrial portion of the United States. Cities and industries draw water supplies from the Ohio and return wastes and domestic sewage. Recently the Cuyahoga River, a tributary of Lake Erie, contained so much floating debris that when the debris was accidentally ignited, the river caught fire. Structures known as "fire breaks" have been built out into the river to fight and control these river fires. Meat packers in St. Joseph, Omaha, Kansas City, and Sioux City dump animal tissue, grease and scum, pieces of animal intestines, and paunch manure directly into the Missouri River without treatment.

Each year, in areas of West Virginia, Kentucky, Ohio, and Pennsylvania, 3½ million tons of acids seep from mines (both active and abandoned) into the nation's streams. Because of this, thousands of miles of flowing water have been made sterile. In the Mississippi River alone, an estimated 50 million fish have been killed since 1958. The U.S. Public Health Service announced in 1964 that the fish kill was caused by two known pesticides, endrin and dieldrin. A Memphis company had been discharging endrin for a great many years into the Mississippi River. The chemical had soaked into the mud and had accumulated to a lethal dose.

Pollution of water comes about in essentially four ways: 1) erosion, 2) industrial operations, 3) heat exchange operations, and 4) domestic sewage.

1) *Erosion*—One of the chief avenues of pollution is the introduction—through improper control of soil in mining, lumbering, and agricultural activities—of erosional products like silt and clay. Turbidity and silt in streams are just as much pollutants as sewage. Erosion is a natural process that has been going on since the beginning of time. But through greed, carelessness, or simple ignorance, our mechanized society has increased the natural rate of erosion beyond com-

prehension or calculation. Each year millions of tons of topsoil are lost from the land, and thousands of miles of once-clean waterways have become rivers of mud. It has been estimated that in the last 200 years, erosion has lowered the entire Mississippi River drainage basin (i.e., from the Appalachians to the Rocky Mountains) by one foot. What results is not just a murky, muddy river. The increased turbidity greatly impairs the penetration of sunlight into the water and thus greatly inhibits the process of photosynthesis upon which all life is based. It also diminishes the precious amounts of oxygen available. The choking load of silt may also directly affect fishes, mussels, and other water-dependent animals by clogging or injuring their gills so that they suffocate.

2) *Industrial Operations*—Industrial operations add a diversity of poisons to water and otherwise make it an uninhabitable environment. Polluting effects from industrial plants are highly varied and may affect aquatic organisms in many different ways. One category of substances includes those that impart disagreeable odors or tastes to the water and impair the human esthetic values of it and the surrounding areas. Another group of substances includes chemicals, such as lead, mercury, phenol and sulfur compounds, and many others that could be directly toxic to all organisms. Brine from oil fields or from phosphate mines causes streams to become highly saline; this alters radically the fauna and flora that inhabit those bodies of water. Many effluents dumped indiscriminately into streams significantly change the pH (the degree of alkalinity or acidity) of the water and cause the types and numbers of aquatic organisms to be reduced sharply.

Many industrial operations are fairly efficient, and they produce only minimal amounts of pollutants. But this is more than balanced by the enormous amounts of water used in various operations; Table I gives several examples.

Table I. Amounts of Water Utilized in Certain Industrial
Processes

Gallons of Water		*Industrial Products*
5		1 gal. of gas
10	Required	1 can of vegetables
25,000	to	1 ton of steel
50,000	Produce	1 ton of paper
600,000		1 ton of synthetic rubber

3) *Heat Exchange Operations*—Many industrial uses of water involve cooling processes that, when dumped back into a stream, can kill much of the life by "thermal pollution." Since nothing was added to it, the water is just as pure as when it was pumped from the river. But the temperature tolerances of many organisms are narrow enough so that thermal pollution may be lethal to them. By raising the temperature of water, it raises the rates of biological processes, which, in turn, require oxygen at a higher rate. Moreover, as the temperature of water is elevated, it holds lesser amounts of oxygen. Severe thermal pollution results in oxygen starvation (suffocation), which kills large numbers of organisms. A rise of 10° may cut in half the survival time of a given organism.

4) *Domestic Sewage*—One of the chief sources of pollution is domestic sewage. The addition of domestic sewage and organic substances often exerts great effects on stream communities, primarily through chemically binding up all of the available oxygen. In situations where dissolved oxygen has been depleted, aerobic bacteria cannot function in decomposition. This process is continued, however, by anaerobic forms and results in the production of such undesirable gases as hydrogen sulfide, ammonia, and methane. These gases further deplete plant and animal life present and contribute to the pollution concentration.

Yet, miraculously enough, streams are capable of cleansing themselves of organic wastes, provided they are given the necessary time and space for this process to operate efficiently. If a stream is dosed with a large amount of sewage, there is a population explosion of bacteria. This results in the dissolved oxygen being totally depleted. Just downstream from the source of pollution, the water may be milky white with accumulated organic matter and huge numbers of decomposers. Only a few other forms of life can possibly live in such conditions. Within a few hundred yards downstream, conditions progressively improve as the sewage becomes more diluted with water. A greater diversity of plants and animals occurs and more oxygen is present for the stream's inhabitants.

Farther downstream, the recovery process continues; the water becomes cleaner and clearer, allowing sunlight to penetrate more deeply; these conditions permit a still greater diversity of plants and animals to inhabit the stream. Eventually, a zone of clean water is attained.

Almost without exception a city locates its water pumping stations upstream and its sewage discharge plants downstream. This strategic location of inflow and outflow plants was historically a logical way to supply the citizens with clean water and to dispose of their wastes. The next city downstream was far enough removed from the upstream sewage discharge plant so that the river or creek could cleanse itself. The distance between the location of one city's discharge and the next city's intake of raw water has become less and less. In today's overpopulated world most streams do not have time to purify themselves, with the result that the cities farther downstream are supplied with progressively more polluted water. In the thirteen-hundred miles of the Ohio River, for instance, the water is used from three to eight times before it joins the Mississippi at Cairo, Illinois.[5]

5. Melvin A. Benarde, *Our Precarious Habitat* (New York: W. W. Norton & Company, 1970), p. 134.

In the past few decades, at least three new kinds of pollutants have begun to choke the waterways. These are household detergents, heavy metals, and various pesticides. Detergents are both a nuisance and a harmful pollutant, especially if they are not degradable. In recent years soap manufacturers have introduced biodegradable detergents, which lessen the harmful effects.

Heavy metals, such as mercury, have been polluting our waters for decades. But only within the last three years have we become aware of the large amounts of mercury in aquatic habitats and its toxicity to aquatic life. Mercury, like arsenic and lead, is a heavy metal and is poisonous to higher animals. The alarming amounts of mercury now in tuna, swordfish, and many other edible fishes pose a very acute threat to man from an economic, biological, and medical standpoint.

Pesticides also pose a serious threat. Many of these synthetic poisons, principally insecticides like DDT, kill not only pests, but a host of other organisms as well. The chief culprits are the chlorinated hydrocarbons and the phosphorus-containing pesticides.

The death of fishes and other forms of aquatic life from acute exposure to unusually high concentrations of pesticides is obviously undesirable. Such occurrences generally are local, readily apparent, and sporadic, with partial or total repopulation occurring quickly. These local "kills" are generally associated with massive runoff from the adjacent land, careless use of pesticides, accidental discharges of industrial wastes, or other accidents.

Widespread, long-term contamination of the environment is much more difficult to evaluate and should be a matter of great public concern. Take, for example, the insecticide DDT. What amounts are harmful or harmless are not precisely known. It is difficult to explain how DDT became so universally distributed in a few short years. It probably reached the oceans via runoff from the land into the rivers.

Marine animals contain inordinately large quantities of DDT even in spite of the tremendous dilution that has certainly occurred as relatively small amounts of DDT reached such a large volume of water as is in the ocean.

DDT, may be absorbed directly or ingested with food. It is then stored, not excreted or metabolized. Undoubtedly, it is passed along the food chain until it reaches higher forms of life, becoming all the while more concentrated.

Water, most assuredly, is one of the most precious renewable resources. The dumping of most of our solid and liquid wastes into our streams, lakes, and oceans cannot continue. An immediate and concerted effort by industries, municipalities, governmental agencies, and many concerned citizens will be necessary to insure clean water for future generations.

SOLID WASTES

If society can solve all the problems of air and water pollution, another major problem, especially in urban areas, will still confront it. This concerns the disposal of solid wastes—the garbage, refuse, rubbish, and trash that are accumulating everywhere. Highways, waterways, and many out-of-the-way places are now huge dumps of mattresses, bottles, bags, paper, cars, cans, refrigerators—the list is endless. The process by which these things break down or degrade is much slower than the rate by which man adds to the enormous, growing garbage dumps.

Biodegradable materials are those that rot, rust, decompose, deteriorate, or in some way break down as a result of the activities of decomposers. Some of the materials that man uses are biologically degradable, but a majority of the things the American consumer uses are non-biodegradable. Non-biodegradable materials include most plastics, polyethylenes, polystyrofoams, metal foils, plastic wraps, aluminum cans, cigarette filters, glass bottles, and the list goes on and on. The trouble is that these things deteriorate exceedingly slowly, if at all. And the materials out of which they are made will not be available by recycling for other uses within the next several thousand years, if then.

The problems of solid wastes demand our urgent attention. One massively important factor is that the U.S. consumer actually consumes very little outside of the food he eats; he just uses things. A variety of things are done to solid wastes, but the materials survive in some form. Technology has added to their longevity and has, undoubtedly, bestowed immortality on such things as plastics and glassware. Each year technology in this country produces (and U.S. consumers dispose of) 55 billion cans, about 30 billion long-lived bottles and jars, and 65 billion metal and plastic bottle caps. Seven million automobiles are junked every year. The average American's annual output of solid waste is about 1,600 lbs., that is, about 4½ pounds per person per day. That adds up to almost 400 million tons of garbage per year. At the current rate of increase, that figure will double in the next twenty years. We Americans will, in 1972, spend about 5 billion dollars to collect and dispose of our garbage.

San Francisco Bay is slowly being filled with trash, garbage, and fill. The same thing is happening to Long Island Sound. Tokyo is using 7,000 tons of garbage every day to fill Tokyo Bay in a desperate attempt to create land for expansion. Staten Island has become a major garbage disposal site and a haven for rats.

For many Americans the problems of solid waste disposal are very simple. Many persons simply throw them away immediately regardless of where they happen to be. They toss them on sidewalks, through car windows, in buildings, parks, and onto lawns. Littering is one of man's more idiotic ecological sins. Every auto campground, every shoulder of every highway, every picnic site tells the story. But littering in the woods goes on far beyond the road's end. A backpack into the Maine woods, a hike down the Appalachian trail, or a ride along the highest ridges of the Rockies shows littering. Even the remotest wilderness areas are affected. Over a seven year period, Sierra Club members hauled 23½ tons of cans and bottles out of wilderness areas in the Sierra mountains. Even the canoe waters of Canada are so heavily used that good housekeeping of camps is breaking down and littering is rampant.

It is becoming universally recognized that current methods of dealing with solid wastes are utterly inadequate. A report by the Department of Health, Education, and Welfare recently labeled 94% of the 12,000 disposal sites in the U.S. as "unacceptable." Many cities are facing disposal crises as population growth simultaneously produces more wastes and reduces the amount of land available for dumping. Many cities have considered having their refuse hauled to distant dumping sites by train. Persons living near the selected sites were not at all happy with the idea, however. Sanitary landfill, where space is available, is a more satisfactory (and expensive) solution than dumping, but it also generates many problems. Water pollution continues, dust pollution is created, and non-biodegradable materials, which do not compact easily, lessen the utility of the fill. Incineration of wastes is another answer; European countries have combined this with power production. Unless great care is taken, however, this answer may merely substitute air pollution for land pollution.

This problem of solid waste disposal is actually a number of problems. The more important ones include the following:

1. Merchants and industries (including grocers, manufacturers, bottlers, suppliers, and general retailers) urgently need to do what they can about the solid waste problem. Merchandise, goods, and foods should be packaged in either returnable or biodegradable containers. An excellent project for interested groups would be to encourage businessmen in one's area to re-evaluate the methods and materials

used in packaging their merchandise. Also, manufacturers ought to be encouraged to overcome their "planned obsolescence" syndrome.

2. The general public needs to be involved in a widespread selective buying campaign. Consumers ought to insist that packaging materials be either returnable or biodegradable. And if they are neither, one can even return them to the merchant and let him dispose of the debris. Milk can be bought in glass returnable bottles, soft drinks in returnable bottles, foods wrapped in see-through polyethylenes can be wrapped in paper, plastic containers ought to be replaced, and foil, plastic wraps, and wax papers should be avoided like the plague.

3. Problems of the sorting of garbage need some attention and action. Individual consumers ought to urge passage of municipal laws making it mandatory that plastics, glass, and other non-biodegradable materials be separated from the degradable materials. We might then be able to recycle more of these materials using differential methods of reclamation.

4. The final disposition of solid wastes deserves careful attention. Each person ought to be supporting legislation and community action designed to dispose more effectively and efficiently of his solid wastes. Minimum air, water, and land pollution and maximum recycling and degradation must be the goals of society.

5. Finally, there is the perennial problem of littering, where one simply and improperly disposes of his trash in the most expeditious manner. An anti-littering behavior necessarily means a change in our individual lifestyles. In the final analysis, in fact, the only solutions to our ecological problems are changes in lifestyles. The litter problem can be minimized by 1) absolutely prohibiting any person, family member, or acquaintance from littering while in our midst, and 2) making a frequent spectacle of ourselves by simply bending over and picking up that piece of paper, can, or any form of debris. If bending over is a spectacle, then each person needs to be spectacular, frequently, every day.

NOISE POLLUTION

The adverse effects of noise are of very recent origin. In 1966 a New York state representative introduced a bill in which he termed excessive noise, "noise pollution." We are being subjected to increasing amounts of noise from jet aircraft, the roar of automobiles and trucks, the blare of TV sets and radios, and the general din of an industrialized, motorized, affluent society. It is already clear that noise can damage hearing: in the United States, insurance compensation claims for loss of hearing have risen to an annual rate in excess of a billion dollars. More than 10 million Americans need hearing aids.

Like other sounds, noise is measured in decibels (db). The faintest sound that can be heard by an adult is at 0 db. At 85 db the danger zone begins and 135 db is the threshold of pain. The following are the decibel equivalents of some common noise-makers: food blender (93), subway train (95), heavy truck (98), power mower (107), motorcycle (110), loud rock music (115), and jet plane at takeoff (150). Clearly, many everyday noises fall in the danger area. As noises in the environment increase, so do hearing deficiencies. It is estimated that 50% of the population in the next twenty years will have some significant hearing impairment. Progressive noise-induced deafness occurs with continuous exposure to sound levels over 80 db.

Noise pollution not only results in deafness, but other physiological symptoms are also attributed to this environmental hazard, including arteriosclerotic heart disease, high blood pressure, psychological disorders, and lack of sleep. Noise pollution is, for the most part, more debilitating than disastrous, but it remains an insidious form of pollution.

A recent manifestation of noise pollution is the sonic boom created by faster-than-sound aircraft. If planes travel faster than 660 miles per hour, an intense pressure wave is generated by the plane. This wave strikes the earth and our ears with a thunderous roar or boom. The plan to produce an American supersonic transport (SST) plane has now been abandoned. This plane would have had the capability of flying at a full speed of 1800 miles per hour. At such speeds, the sonic boom would be very intense and would have inconvenienced and bothered millions of persons in this country. This disastrous potentiality alone should have been enough to halt development of it.

RADIATION

An atomic blast near the center of Hiroshima, Japan, on August 6, 1945, ushered in the Atomic Age. This event and its technological ramifications have grossly altered the political, military, sociological, and economic outlooks of all of humanity. One other important aspect of the atomic technology is the environmental effects of the ensuing radiation. Many positive and beneficial effects have resulted from this atomic knowledge. The benefits to the military, to research, and to medicine are, indeed, enormous. Here, only the environmental hazards associated with radiation will be considered.

All persons experience some natural radiation throughout their entire lives. This "background" radiation comes from the sun, the earth, and cosmic rays. It is in the air one breathes, the water one drinks, and the food one eats. Only the additional radiation that man has experienced since 1945 by man-made nuclear reactions will be considered.

Many chemically unstable elements decay with time. The decay process is accomplished by the loss or radiation of various types of highly energized rays (alpha, beta, gamma, and x-rays). These rays, upon striking organisms, cause varying degrees of damage that may result in physical, chemical, or biological changes; this is termed *ionizing radiation*. Radiation is measured in terms of the damage the dose evokes.

Ionizing radiation is one of those environmental hazards that man cannot directly sense. It cannot be seen, heard, felt, touched, or tasted. There is no sensation of pain, warmth, or vibration that accompanies even a lethal dosage. We must, therefore, rely upon rather sophisticated devices to inform us of dangerous levels of radiation. The question of what constitutes a dangerous amount of radiation or what amount is "harmless" cannot be answered simply. The nature of the radiation, its source and intensity, the duration of the exposure, its point of impact on an organism, and the individual susceptibility to ionizing radiation are all involved in determining the effect of the dosage. Certainly, even the smallest amounts of radiation have no beneficial effects on organisms, and even minute amounts can cause physiological or genetic problems. Thus, environmental, man-made radiation is to be avoided wherever possible.

Radiation is added to the biosphere principally by atmospheric atomic or thermonuclear blasts. Other sources would include debris from small nuclear weapons, waste products from power reactors, and many other miscellaneous peaceful uses of atomic energy. The most common environmental forms of radiation are found in fallout from nuclear detonations; the most important ones include isotopes (forms) of strontium (strontium-90), cesium (cesium-137), zinc (zinc-65), and cobalt (cobalt-60). Great quantities of radioactive substances are ejected by nuclear detonations and are caught up by air currents, distributed globally, and subsequently deposited on land and water. These substances then get into organisms via food chains or biogeochemical cycles and are distributed throughout an ecosystem.

Strontium-90 is probably the one environmental form of radioactivity that has caused the most concern in recent years. It is one of the most common components of atomic fallout and it persists for a very long time. Its half-life (the time for one-half of the radiation to be dissipated) is about thirty years. Strontium behaves biogeochemically very much like calcium and can be readily absorbed by plants. Strontium-90 is transmitted to man in cow's milk and via various cereals. Like calcium, it is deposited in bone in close proximity to tissues making blood. Such tissues are very sensitive to radiation, and strontium-90 has been known to induce certain severe or lethal blood abnormalities.

Most of the other radioactive pollutants are absorbed either through the leaves or roots of plants and thereby enter into food chains. Because of the concentrating effects of organisms, their influences become increasingly manifested the higher they go in a food chain. And because man represents the apex of many food chains, the effects on human populations are greater than on the populations of other animals or plants.

The effects of radiation on man run the spectrum from no immediate or attributable effect to almost instant death. Since the latter occurs at or near a blast or in connection with a severe accident, such events are, thankfully, quite rare.

But the continuous effects of low level radiation in the biosphere warrant some treatment here.

Radiation can manifest itself in a variety of ways, principally as it affects 1) prenatal and infant mortality, and 2) heredity and aging. Many reports have indicated that certain prenatal effects are associated with radiation. Prenatal radiation has been correlated with increased incidence of leukemia, certain cancers, and an increase in infant mortality from all sources. One report stated that in the 1960's, one-third of all infant deaths in their first year of life may have been attributable to the effects of strontium-90. Because of the inherent difficulties of studying both pre- and post-natal effects, the true effects of radiation damage are not, at this time, known.

Radiation can cause some long-term influences on future populations by altering the genetic material. Radiation is known to induce genetic mutations or chromosomal alterations that are passed along to subsequent generations. Thus, radiation damage may not be readily apparent for one to several generations. Other hypotheses have been advanced proposing that there is a correlation between radiation and the rate of aging. Although no clear-cut statements can be made at this time, there are indications that radiation does lead to an earlier breakdown of cellular integrity, a decrease in rate of cell production, and other manifestations characteristic of aging.

Environmental radiation effects are not fully known at this time. Man may not be in the midst of a radiation crisis, but certainly no one wants to see the levels of radiation increase further. Careful controls on thermonuclear power plants and on the disposal of radioactive wastes are essential for the protection of life. But the consuming concern for humanity is that everyone do everything possible to prevent even a limited thermonuclear war. In addition to all the human lives that would be lost, such a holocaust could permanently poison all ecosystems.

Pollution of the biosphere and its ecosystems represents some of man's most severe problems. A pristine environment is not possible, but neither can man continue to live with increasing amounts of garbage, debris, filth, gases, and dirt in his surroundings. The technological know-how to resolve many of the sources of environmental pollution is now available. But the solutions will be inconceivably costly. Is society ready to shoulder the enormous financial burden of the restoration of the environment? As someone said, "It's your money *or* your life!"

Chapter Three

Population
Explosion

Certainly *the* most important manifestation of the environmental crisis is the phenomenal rate of increase in numbers of humans. The size of the human population has exploded within the last two centuries and has reached critical proportions. Science and the whole of society must seek immediate, valid, workable solutions to this enormous human problem, which is at the root of most of the other environmental problems. It is, therefore, fitting that considerable attention be devoted in this volume to population growth and to the associated parameters of the "population bomb."

POPULATION GROWTH

First, the dynamics of population growth will be explored, and then attention will be given specifically to problems relating to the growth of the human species. A *population* is defined as a group of organisms all of which are essentially alike (i.e., they all belong to the same species). In our example of a pond ecosystem, there are many different populations of insects, phytoplankton, fishes, clams, bacteria, and rooted plants—all of which are involved in various ways in the functioning of the ecosystem. A given population has certain characteristics that are not features of the individuals within the group, but are unique to the population as a whole. Some of these population features are dispersion, density, and rates of birth and death.

If one considers populations of houseflies or oak trees or lions or amoebae, one obvious characteristic of these and all populations is their ability to reproduce. Indeed, the ability to produce a subsequent generation is a basic and fundamental feature of all organisms. In fact, most organisms are especially adept at it. A given bacterium, for example, will reproduce about every twenty minutes under optimum conditions; each bacterial cell divides to form two new organisms. If conditions remain optimum, a single bacterium will, in twenty-four hours, leave a mass of progeny weighing in excess of 2,000 tons! A female housefly may lay about 850 eggs during one year. If every egg hatched and if all females laid at the same rate, the seventh generation would contain in excess of 6 trillion flies. Or consider the reproductive potential of a parasite like the human liver fluke. Each parasite (all flukes contain both male and female reproductive organs) may produce up to 10 million offspring each year as a maximum potential. Assuming all survived and each reproduced, we would soon be literally "up to our ears" in flukes.

These three examples clearly illustrate the reproductive capabilities of organisms. All other organisms show the same high reproductive potential. This reproductive (biotic) potential is an inherent property of a population and is invariably reflected as a geometric (or logarithmic) increase in numbers. Such growth rates are achieved by repeated doubling of the population size. Ecologists talk almost reverently of the *intrinsic rate of natural increase,* the reproductive capacity of a population under ideal conditions.

Logarithmic growth patterns stagger the imagination. A story illustrating it is told of an enterprising young man seeking work. He persuaded his employer to allow him to work for only one cent the first day, two cents the next day, four cents the third day, eight cents the fourth day, and so on. The young man's pay for the fifteenth day was more than

$160, while that for his twenty-fifth day was in excess of $167,000. Had the employer remained in business, he would have paid his new employee wages of more than 10 million dollars for the month.[1] Repeated doubling, even from a very minute base, results in astronomical figures within a short period of time.

Still, one can easily observe that man is not really being overrun by bacteria, houseflies, flukes, or any other organism. Obviously, opposing forces are operating to hold population growth in check. These forces are collectively referred to as *environmental resistance*. They include any and all chemical, physical, and biological factors in the environment that tend to limit population size. Limitations in food supply, nutrients, and living space, or increases in competition, parasitism, and rate of dying are but a few examples. This is shown in the equation,

$$A - B = C,$$

where A is the theoretical reproductive potential, B represents the effects of environmental resistance, and C is the actual observed population size.

The size of a population will be determined by a ratio of its birth rate to its death rate. Environmental resistance factors can either lower the birth rate or increase the death rate. If natality and mortality rates are equal to each other, no change in population will occur. But if there is an increase in birth rate over death rate, then population will increase; the reverse is true when death rates exceed birth rates.

It is important that the interactions of reproductive potential and environmental resistance be clearly understood. If a small number of organisms of any population is introduced into a new area with conditions ideal for growth, the population will increase with time. Figure 7 illustrates the pattern

1. Paul R. Ehrlich and Anne H. Ehrlich, *Population, Resources, Environment* (San Francisco: W. H. Freeman and Company, 1970), p. 41.

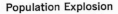

Population Explosion

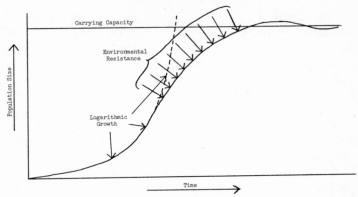

FIGURE 7. *Growth of a population illustrating the J-shaped and the S-shaped growth curves.*

of growth of the hypothetical population. Growth in numbers proceeds slowly at first, but soon the rate dramatically increases by logarithmic proportions. The optimum conditions for growth would be reflected in maximum reproductive activity and minimum environmental resistance. Quite obviously, the rate of growth cannot continue to increase indefinitely; within a short period of time, the growth rate would be astronomical, the population doubling time becoming instantaneous.

The growth rate of a population typically slows down after a while. This may be due to diminishing food supplies, increased competition, reduction in available nutrients, increased mortality of the young, or a thousand other causes. At any rate, environmental resistance begins to affect the rate of growth, and continues to do so until significant increase is no longer possible. Thus, natality and mortality become equal and the rate of growth is zero.

The point at which additional organisms cannot be supported by the ecosystem is termed the *carrying capacity*. This is the maximum number of organisms in a population that the ecosystem can support, given its physical and biological limitations. Population can and usually does vary somewhat around this point, but it can never exceed this level for long or in significantly large numbers. If population were to exceed the carrying capacity, the death rate would soon become greater than the birth rate and a level of stability would eventually be reached at or near the carrying capacity.

Many different environmental factors may be involved in determining the carrying capacity of an ecosystem for a given population. The intensity of many environmental resistance factors increases as density of population increases. These density-dependent factors include such things as available food, living space, competition, and predation. These act like governors on an engine in that the higher the rate of increase, the more intense are their effects on impeding growth. Other environmental resistance factors operate altogether independently of the numbers of organisms present. Such density-independent factors would include rainfall, changes in temperature, length of the daylight hours, and many other climatic factors.

Figure 7 illustrates two different types of growth curves that can be observed in nature. One type is characterized by logarithmic growth that continues until some factor in the environment suddenly becomes limiting. The curve of such a type has a J-shape in its acceleration phase. Populations of certain species of algae, bacteria, insects, annual plants, certain rodents, and man (during the past millennium) exhibit a J-shaped pattern. Obviously, such a growth pace cannot continue for long. Instead of leveling off, there is a precipitous decrease in numbers due to an eventual, sudden, massive decline in population.

The other type is termed the sigmoid or S-shaped growth curve. Perhaps a majority of populations exhibit this second pattern. Studies on small aquatic organisms, birds, mammals, and many other plants and animals have shown that most species illustrate the S-shaped curve. Such a growth pattern initially is like the J-shaped curve, but soon the rate of increase begins to slow down. Environmental resistance becomes increasingly influential as population approaches the carrying capacity.

All growth studies to date clearly indicate that population cannot continue to increase indefinitely. A degree of stability is inevitably imposed upon uncontrolled growth. These checks may be manifested abruptly, as in the J-shaped curve, or gradually, as illustrated by the S-shaped curve. Many intrinsic and extrinsic forces are instrumental in establishing a degree of population equilibrium. What follows is a consideration of the growth of one population (that of *Homo sapiens*) and a fuller exploration of its explosion.

HUMAN POPULATION

The human species is a very new evolutionary form; it appeared only about 2 million years ago. No substantial data is available on numbers prior to the agricultural revolution of about 8000 B.C. and only scanty information prior to the first census taken in the 1600's. It has been estimated that the population was about 5 million at 8,000 B.C.[2] The total human population at the time of Christ is estimated to have been about 250 million. By the year 1650, that number had doubled. Just 180 years later, in 1830, it had doubled again. It doubled once more over the next century, so that by 1930 the population was 2 billion. By 1975-1977, the population will have doubled again and we will have 4 billion neighbors. Figure 8 illustrates this phenomenal increase.

Clearly, the growth of the human population is increasing logarithmically. Since the beginning of the Christian era, the time necessary for the population to double has dwindled from 1650 years to 180 years to 100 years to 45-47 years. The world's population is now growing at the unprecedented

2. *Ibid.*, p. 5.

rate of 2% per year, and the human species is doubling its numbers every thirty-five years. At that rate, in about seventy years (year 2045), there will be 16 billion persons, and by the year 2150 (about 180 years hence), there will be 128 billion souls. In 1,000 years, there should be a billion billion persons, or about 1,700 persons per square yard of the entire earth's surface, both land and sea.[3] If each reader of these words were reproducing at a rate of 2% per annum, in 1000 years each reader would have 300 million living descendants.

If it is assumed that each person lives the Biblical life span of three score and ten years, and the present population doubling time is thirty-five years, think of the dramatic changes that will have occurred in one's lifetime. The population will have quadrupled during this time. As each person approaches his seventieth birthday, each individual will have only one-fourth of the food, living space, water, shelter, available energy, and minerals that were available to him at birth.

The concerns about the human growth patterns are not exclusively those of the current century. In the year 1798, a now-famous theologian, economist, and demographer named Thomas Robert Malthus wrote discerningly about human growth. In *An Essay On the Principle of Population,*[4] Malthus raised some very important points about the human population. He wrote that unchecked population growth increases in a geometrical (logarithmical) ratio, but that subsistence (food, principally) increases only in an arithmetical ratio. In other words the geometric increase would be 1, 2, 4, 8, 16, 32, 64, 128, 256, 512 while the arithmetic increase would be 1, 2, 3, 4, 5, 6, 7, 8, 9, 10. Malthus clearly perceived that the number of humans could not increase

3. *Ibid.,* p. 41.
4. Thomas Robert Malthus, "An Essay on the Principle of Population," in *Population, Evolution, and Birth Control,* ed. by Garrett Hardin (2nd ed.; San Francisco: W. H. Freeman and Company, 1969), pp. 4–16.

indefinitely (i.e., in the J-shaped pattern) but must level out because of the limitations of subsistence (i.e., exhibit an S-shaped curve). He wrote that many other factors would help curb the increase in human population, among them wars, epidemics, plagues, and famines. In modern jargon, these would be forms of environmental resistance and would primarily increase mortality rates.

The spectacular increase in population size during the past 200 years has not really borne out Malthus's dire predictions of the means by which population can be controlled. Wars have not been significant in depressing the growth of world population. Famines and the effects of diseases have been somewhat more effective, but the population has grown dramatically in spite of them. How can the enormous differences be accounted for between what would be normally expected from the growth of the human population (S-shaped curve) and what has actually happened (J-shaped curve)?

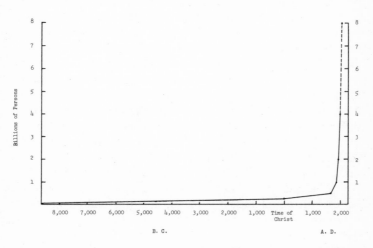

FIGURE 8. *The growth curve of the human population from 8000 B.C. to present, and projected growth until the year A.D. 2010.*

Man has used his superior mental ability in order to alter the natural forces that would have suppressed population growth. Man has evolved to the point where he can alter or modify his surroundings. In so doing, he has temporarily minimized or suspended the environmental resistance that would have inhibited population growth. To repeat, *man has been able to temporarily suspend environmental resistance* that would have produced for our population an S-shaped growth curve. Such a remarkable feat has no precedent in the long evolution of life.

This enormous feat has been accomplished by practicing death control. This does not mean that man's activities are causing people to die; the reverse is true. Society has invested huge sums of money and innumerable persons and their collective expertise to save and prolong lives. Society has been practicing death control by trying to eliminate it or to push it as far into the future as possible. The entire medical and paramedical professions are committed to the saving of lives and the promotion of health. The dental, pharmaceutical, public health, nutritional, and related professions have added immeasurably to the eradication of diseases and the minimization of many forms of human suffering.

The result of our efficient health services has been to increase the longevity of as many individuals as possible. Man has been able to achieve this by circumventing many different forms of environmental resistance. Natural forms of environmental resistance include cholera, diphtheria, polio, infirmities, accidents, malaria, appendicitis, heart diseases, and many others. Technology has increased food yields, added to our various creature comforts, produced a better nutritional base for many, and has eliminated many environmental threats to our survival. *Homo sapiens* now lives better and longer than ever before.

Most persons want to live as long as they can contribute meaningfully to society. Do not misconstrue that the above statements imply that the author is against medical progress. But it is important to understand that medical science has postponed the impacts of environmental resistance until later in life. Death of any organism, including man, is inevitable, and modern scientific technology can succeed only in *temporarily* minimizing the finality of environmental resistance. As Boughey has stated, "This dramatic and universal reduction in mortality rates throughout the world in the 1950's is the most significant individual causal factor of the present population explosion."[5]

BIRTH AND DEATH RATES

The spectacular growth of the human population during the last 200 years has been a result of an imbalance in the ratio of birth rates and death rates. It is true that average family size has decreased during this period, and even the birth rate has decreased. But the death rate has not been permitted to keep pace with the decreasing birth rate.

The birth and death rates will now be explored for the human population. Both rates are computed on the basis of numbers of births or deaths per thousand individuals of the population. For example, in 1971 in the United States, there was an average of 18.2 births per 1000 citizens. During the same year, there was, on the average, 9.3 deaths per 1000 of the population. A subtraction of the number of deaths from the number of births indicates a net increase in 1971 of 8.9 persons per thousand. For demographic purposes, this figure is adjusted upward to eleven per thousand to account for age structure, emigrations, life expectancies, and a number of other computations. The percentage growth for the U.S. was 1.1% in 1971. If this were a constant rate, this country's

5. Arthur S. Boughey, *Man and the Environment* (New York: Macmillan Company, 1971), p. 243.

population would double in about 63 years, or by the year A.D. 2035.[6]

A growth rate of 1.1% per year is comparatively low since the world's population is growing at 2.0% per year. Clearly, populations in other parts of the world are growing at a considerably higher rate than that in this country. Kuwait, for example, has a growth rate of 8.2%; Costa Rica, 3.8%; Mexico, Honduras, and Columbia, 3.4%; and India, 2.6%. Thirty-six of the 145 countries listed have growth rates of 3.0% or higher. The average growth rates for some continents are Latin America, 2.9%; Africa, 2.7%; and Asia, 2.3%. On the other hand, Europe has a very low rate of growth with an average rate of about 0.8% which makes the populations of European countries much more stable than those of other parts of the world. The rates of a few other selected countries are Canada, 1.7%; mainland China, 1.8%; West Germany, 0.4%; United Kingdom, 0.5%; and U.S.S.R., 1.0%.[7]

To summarize, changes in population are due mainly to the imbalance between birth and death rates. Birth rates have declined during the last 200 years, especially in those countries where the per capita income, levels of education, and degree of industrialization have risen. But because of the tremendous advances of medicine, nutrition, and hygiene, the death rates have fallen much faster. And so the entire world is experiencing a population boom. The fundamental questions are these: 1) What is the optimum number of people that the world can support? 2) How can population stability be achieved?

In ecological considerations the optimum population is that of the carrying capacity of our planet. No one can quantify this exactly because of the different standards of living.

6. *1971 World Population Data Sheet*, Population Reference Bureau, Washington, D.C., Revised August, 1971.
7. *Ibid.*

lifestyles, behavioral mores, and degree of development of the various countries. It is certainly clear, however, that if middle-class America is taken as the standard, it is lower than the current global population. This country has about 6% of the world's population and consumes roughly 50% of the world's resources. It is economically, materially, and physically impossible to support the world's 1972 population of approximately 3.8 billion in the manner to which the average American is accustomed. The hypothesis that all persons can live at the level of a middle-class American is simply invalid, given the current demographic trends.

Perhaps the world could support a world population of 3.8 billion persons *if* everyone's standard of living were considerably lower than that of the average American. If the world's resources were shared equally, then everyone could live at a level $\frac{1}{4}$ or $\frac{1}{10}$ or $\frac{1}{100}$ that of the typical American of 1972. (Precise data are difficult to come by to predict the per capita standard of living for all persons.) Hulett writes that using the current living standards in the U.S. as a criterion, the optimum world population would be about 1 billion persons.[8] This is a startling statistic when one considers that the present size of the world's population is 3.8 billion persons. Using this frame of reference, the earth is already overpopulated by almost 300%!

The second question, "How can man achieve population stability?" is equally difficult to answer. It is clear that population growth cannot continue for long in its logarithmic acceleration; it is impossible for the J-shaped curve to be extended indefinitely. The human population must soon experience a phenomenon known as zero population growth (ZPG). This means that birth and death rates must be brought into equilibrium in order to achieve a stable, constant population. This can be accomplished voluntarily by

8. H. R. Hulett, "Optimum World Population," *Bioscience,* 20 (February 1, 1970), pp. 160–161.

man, or nature will impose ZPG on him, eventually, invariably, and harshly. The fundamental question is whether man can impose the necessarily severe and rigid population controls on himself, or whether he will simply let nature do it for him. The humane way, of course, is that of man; the most efficient way is that of nature. A discussion of both ways follows.

Naturally occurring checks on population have been referred to earlier. Many of the effects of disease, pestilence, infirmities, and abnormalities have been circumvented by modern medical, hygienic, and pharmacological technology. But the one natural limitation mankind cannot avoid is the food crisis. The Malthusian ideas of the ability to feed a burgeoning population increasing only arithmetically still hold. The logarithmic population growth will exceed the arithmetic subsistence rate at some point in time. The timing of this crucially important meeting of two lines on a graph is not in the distant future, but occurred some fifteen years ago! The Paddock brothers have stated very plainly that in the year 1958, "The stork . . . passed the plow."[9]

Humanity is rushing headlong into a massive, world-wide famine. Enormous numbers of persons will certainly starve in the next fifteen years, especially in South America, Africa, and Asia. The Paddock brothers use an interesting metaphor:

> A locomotive is roaring full throttle down the track. Just around the bend an impenetrable mudslide has oozed across the track. There it lies, inert, static, deadly. Nothing can stop the locomotive in time. Collision is inevitable. Catastrophe is foredoomed. Miles back up the track the locomotive could have been warned and stopped. Years ago the mud-soaked hill could have been shored up to forestall the land slide. Now it is too late. The locomotive roaring straight at us is the population explosion. The unmovable landslide across the

9. William Paddock and Paul Paddock, *Famine-1975! America's Decision: Who Will Survive?* (Boston: Little, Brown and Company, 1967), p. 44.

tracks is the stagnant production of food in the under-developed nations, the nations where the population increases are the greatest. The collision is inevitable. The famines are inevitable.[10]

The inevitability of famine is a sobering idea, but all indications are that famine will be the ultimate form of environmental resistance to curb population growth. A quick review of the ideas expressed in Chapter I concerning thermodynamics, energy flow, and food chains will substantiate the cruciality of a finite amount of food energy. Ecologically, our current food crisis was evident long ago, but humanity obviously did not heed the warning cries of ecologists, demographers, and many others.

The food shortages and the ensuing famine are inevitable unless some dramatic developments occur, and developments of the magnitude that will be required are very unlikely. Precise timing of when the famine will reach disastrous proportions range from 1975 to 1980-84 to 1985.[11] Even the most optimistic experts indicate that there will be a worldwide food disaster by the year 1990. The effects of this impending disaster will not be felt uniformly in all countries. Those underdeveloped will be hardest hit. Such countries are characterized by rapid growth rates, low degree of industrialization, inefficient agricultural methods, a high degree of illiteracy, poverty, and other related problems. The peoples of these countries are already starving. The nations in question include most of those in South America, Africa, and Asia. By contrast, the developed countries are those in which the degrees of affluence, industrialization, education, and nutrition are rather high, and those in which the growth rate is fairly low—countries in North America and Europe, along with Japan, Australia, and Russia.[12] Underdeveloped

10. *Ibid.,* pp. 8–9.
11. Boughey, *op. cit.,* p. 265.
12. Paul R. Ehrlich, *The Population Bomb* (New York: Ballantine Books, 1968), p. 22.

countries like India are moving very rapidly toward an increased dependence upon developed countries for food; their demands are already enormous and will soon be gigantic.

Many reports state that half the world's population was already underfed or malnourished in 1971. And if the population doubles in the next thirty-five years, the food supplies will simply not be sufficient to provide everyone even a minimum amount. An estimated 1.9 billion persons are hungry today; in 35 years, that figure will be 3.8 billion.

Insufficient food produces a number of other related conditions that can cause death. Malnourishment results in lowered resistance to most infectious and parasitic diseases. Food deficiencies can also cause a higher incidence of infant mortality, diarrhea, marasmus and kwashiorkor (both of which are a result of protein deficiencies), beriberi, anemia, rickets, scurvy, and so on. Hunger, with all its attendant conditions, is indeed a tragedy for humanity. As long as the population remains as large as it is today, hunger will be a constant companion for about one-half of all humanity.

Humanity today faces a bleak future in which the population, especially in certain areas, will experience severe and massive die-offs due to famine. From an ecological, economic, and agricultural viewpoint, the famine is inevitable. It cannot be postponed for long. It will be the world's greatest catastrophe to date.

FOOD PRODUCTIVITY

Is there any hope at all? Does humanity have a future? Can we delay the crushing effects of the famine? How can the growing problems of acute hunger, especially in the underdeveloped countries, be minimized? Can science and technology bail humanity out of this dilemma? What are the faint glimmers of hope (if there are any)?

Certainly technology ought to seek out new ways of increasing food productivity. If some new breakthroughs develop, man will have bought himself some additional time before the real onslaught occurs. Some new ideas and a lot of myths have developed about new sources of food; perhaps some evaluation of the more popular ones should be made here.

Improving agricultural yields is often mentioned as a panacea for the food problems. It goes under the popular nomenclature of the "green revolution." It was hoped by some that a transformation of agricultural practices might keep food production well ahead of people production. This green revolution was based on a number of new developments, including 1) the development of new high-yield crops, particularly rice, wheat, corn, and other grains; 2) irrigation of heretofore arid lands to convert them into grain-producing areas; 3) massive uses of fertilizers to elevate productivity; and 4) land reform, in which acreage is returned by governments to individual workers.

There are inherent difficulties with each of the four legs upon which the green revolution stands. The development of "miracle" rice and wheat requires an enormous amount of prior agricultural research. Such agrarian research requires time, and an abundance of time is simply not available. The potential new strains require certain climatic conditions, large amounts of fertilizer, careful isolation against a plethora of pests, blights, and parasites, and acceptance by the natives who must plant, cultivate, and then consume the crops. The chances of all these things happening in concert are remote.

Irrigation initially appears to be a profitable route, except that it is prohibitively expensive, especially in rolling terrain. And in the 1970's, usable water is not abundantly available. Fertilizers also enhance productivity, but they modify, on a grand scale, the natural biogeochemical cycles. Fertilizers are expensive to manufacture, transport, and to introduce to the natives. Not all persons are convinced of the benefits of fertilizers, and not all soils will produce significantly larger amounts after being fertilized. Land reform is perhaps a move in the right direction, but to implement it would require a great deal of time in which to change certain political, economic, and agricultural outlooks.

The so-called "green revolution," accompanied by very unusual and unexpectedly favorable weather conditions, has improved the agricultural yields of certain areas of the planet during the last five years. Many food experts feel that the increased yields were only temporary, and that over a decade or two, the yields will not have been significantly increased. At best, the green revolution has bought some time, but not enough time to solve the problems of famine and those of the exploding population. According to Paddock, the green revolution is neither very green nor very revolutionary.[13] The revolution that must precede any great food or agricultural transformation will have to be preceded itself by a revolution of population control.

Until recently many persons felt that mankind could turn to the oceans and find there enormous quantities of both food and mineral riches. Extensive harvesting of food and the mining of minerals from the sea are, for the most part, cruel myths. Perhaps this developed as a result of ambitious projections of the yields of fishes, plankton, algae, and the like. The resources of the seas have been exaggerated, and the costs of harvesting them have been wholly underestimated. Even if man tried to harvest the oceans, he runs the danger of overexploitation of them by excessive fishing, harvesting, or mining. Such activities could severely reduce the oxygen production, energy flow, and biogeochemical cycles upon which all of life, both terrestrial and aquatic, so intimately depends.

Some other nontraditional sources have been proposed, but all have a limited potential. Some of these are desaliniza-

13. William C. Paddock, "How Green is the Green Revolution?" *Bioscience* 20 (August 15, 1970), pp. 897–902.

tion of sea water for irrigation, consumption, or hydroponics (the practice of growing plants in a soil-less or watery culture); raising bacteria and fungi on petroleum or other substances; the harvesting of grass or leaves; and the development of new synthetic foods. The best known of the substitute or synthetic foods is Incaparina. It is a blend of corn and cottonseed meal fortified with certain vitamins. Its adoption in Central America is less than overwhelming due to its texture and bland taste.

Letting nature have its way, that is, allowing natural forms of environmental resistance to exert themselves, is not a very pleasant solution to overpopulation, and the looming famine, with all its related horrors, should be minimized wherever possible. What about the human control of population? Is this a more acceptable mode of approaching a bleak future? What are the avenues open to *Homo sapiens* for population control?

POPULATION CONTROL

Population control is the regulation by society of the size of the human population. Population control can be accomplished by either increasing mortality, reducing natality, or a combination of both. Although increasing the mortality rate is not an acceptable means for most people, it is one option open to society. The preferred method is by regulating the natality rate.

The preferred methods of birth control are those that are accepted voluntarily by society. It is absolutely essential that the existing means of birth control, plus additional measures that research might evolve in the next few years, be made universally available. A number of conventional methods are now available, including intrauterine devices and contraceptive pills.

More liberal public policies with regard to abortion should be developed. Some persons look with disfavor upon abortion, especially if employed not as a therapeutic action but as an alternate means of birth control. It is just as bad, however, if not worse, to force an unwanted pregnancy upon females. Persons are questioning the justice of many of our current abortion laws on the ground that they infringe upon the rights of females. The American Civil Liberties Union has charged that many of our existing abortion laws are unconstitutional since they are based by and large on the teachings of one Christian group, the Roman Catholic Church. Roman Catholicism's stands on abortion and birth control are clearly away from the mainstream of the rest of society, including both religious and secular sectors. Its dogmatic position on these matters must not be permitted to determine civil legislation governing other American citizens who do not share its religious views. Abortion is not the answer to birth control since it involves both the competing claims of an unborn fetus and the potential dangers of either a physiological or psychological trauma to the female. It must be legally available as a last resort when contraceptives fail to prevent an unwanted pregnancy.

Other voluntary measures for birth control include the various means of sterilization. Sterilizations now can be reversed in a rather high percentage of cases in both males and females. Vasectomy, the cutting and tying off the sperm tube (*vas deferens*) in males, has become an increasingly popular means of reducing fertility. Future research may result in a wide variety of mechanical, chemical, and hormonal methods by which conception can be prevented.

If voluntary measures for limiting the natality rate are not sufficient to achieve ZPG, society may impose strict, involuntary measures on itself. Within a few years, rigid compulsory methods will be advocated to protect humanity from total destruction by overpopulation. A number of compulsory ideas have been proposed. Chemicals that temporarily sterilize could be added to municipal water supplies or to staple foods. Compulsory sterilization has been advocated for both mothers and fathers after having two or three children.

Economic incentives have been proposed to assist in birth control. Ideas regarding changes in tax laws, child support, and welfare benefits are often suggested. Childless persons might be given some income tax relief coupled with harsh increases in taxes for having more than a set number of children. Monies available for child support and as welfare benefits could be withheld because of excessive births. Incentives could also be in the form of monetary payments made to married couples who refrain from producing children in a particular time interval (i.e., for achieving nonpregnancy).

Educational campaigns can also contribute meaningfully to reducing natality. Sex education, family planning, and the use of all forms of communications media can be effective. Excellent reviews of the methods of population control, both voluntary and involuntary, have been developed by Boughey[14] and Ehrlich and Ehrlich.[15] The problems of birth control are exceedingly complex and have far-reaching ethical ramifications. Effective birth control will involve profoundly important economic, sociological, political, medical, religious, and ecological changes. In short, a change in our lifestyles will be required in order to enable ZPG to occur both effectively and ethically.

The decade of the 1970's promises to be the most crucial ten years in our long history. During this time we must begin to develop as well as to put into practice valid, workable solutions to our ecological problems, especially those pertaining to population control. The urgency of finding answers cannot be overemphasized.

For the first time in the history of the life sciences, biologists and ecologists are beginning to raise some very pro-

14. Boughey, *op. cit.,* pp. 289–311.
15. Ehrlich and Ehrlich, *op. cit.,* pp. 211–57.

found questions. Environmental concerns are extending into areas of theology, ethics, and morality. Scientists see the urgency of establishing priorities on the many problems that confront us. What humanity needs is human and effective guidance as man continues through this decade with its morass of problems.

The Church has a unique opportunity to help meet the urgent challenges in human ecology posed by the life sciences. The collective insights of theology, philosophy, and ethics are desperately needed. Business cannot continue as usual. The problems are enormous and time is short.

CATASTROPHE AND ECSTASY

H. Paul Santmire

Preface

A number of years ago a friend asked me to join one of Timothy Leary's first groups at Harvard in some experimentation with LSD. I declined the invitation, mainly because my studies in the theology of nature were consuming so much of my time and energy. I have no way of knowing, of course, what would have happened had I accepted my friend's invitation. But I do know that the course I did follow, that rather dry academic commitment of fifteen years ago, was the beginning of a profound existential experience, with deep moments of fear and horror, as well as the "highs" of joy and hope.

The fear and the horror. The world is at present heading toward an ecological catastrophe. That is the testimony of a wide spectrum of responsible scientists. Increasingly, the thought of the planetary crisis we are now facing has been giving me waking nightmares. Think of the oft-quoted words of Yeats:

Things fall apart; the center cannot hold;
Mere anarchy is loosed upon the world,
The blood-dimmed tide is loosed, and everywhere
The ceremony of innocence is drowned;
The best lack all conviction, while the worst
Are full of passionate intensity.

The more I have reflected upon the ecological crisis today,

the more words such as these have floated through my consciousness.[1]

The joy and the hope. Perhaps because of my growing apocalyptic mood, perhaps for other reasons, during the past fifteen years the biblical proclamation of the new heavens and the new earth has more and more come to captivate my mind and heart as I have worked on my own lifestyle and tried to develop my own thinking. So another poetic image has been constantly before me, this one created by Hopkins—writing about the same time as Yeats—in "God's Grandeur":

Generations have trod, have trod, have trod;
  And all is seared with trade; bleared, smeared with toil;
  And wears man's smudge and shares man's smell; the soil
Is bare now, nor can foot feel, being shod.

And for all this, nature is never spent;
  There lives the dearest freshness deep down things;
And though the last lights off the black West went
  Oh, morning, at the brown brink eastward, springs—
Because the Holy Ghost over the bent
  World broods with warm breast and with ah! bright wings.

The vision of wholeness and renewal for all things—this I am seeing more clearly with the passing of each day.

Having seen the blood-dimmed tide and the dearest freshness deep down things, I sense that I have been hallucinating without drugs. I want to describe some of these "hallucinations." I want to tell about my "trip," with the hope that the reader will respond with some visionary thinking and action of his own.

1. In addition to Paul Lutz's essay in the first half of this volume, see the comprehensive study by Richard A. Falk, *Our Endangered Planet: Prospects and Proposals For Survival* (New York: Random House, 1971). For a convenient summary of the literature, see the review by Paul Shepard, *New York Times Book Review*, Feb. 21, 1971. See also *The Environmental Handbook*, ed. Garrett de Bell (New York: Ballantine Books, 1970); and, still worth consulting, Harrison Brown, *The Challenge of Man's Future* (New York: Viking Press, 1954).

What follows is an essay in practical theology. Practical theology is that passionate first-person-singular kind of religious discourse that is the boundary line between substantive theological reflection and the concrete religious life. Practical theology draws on the work of biblical, historical, dogmatic, and apologetic theology. It depends on the discipline of theological ethics (social and personal). And it is intimately related to the various analyses and syntheses of the theology of culture. Presupposing all these forms of critical and constructive theology, practical theology seeks to challenge, sensitize, and inspire. Its goal, therefore, is not to say anything final about anything, but to engage the reader with pressing theological issues in order to lead him or her to some open avenues for further and deeper reflection, and to encourage commitment to more resolute and more responsible patterns of action.

With regard specifically to the analyses of the theology of culture, I want to emphasize that the following essay presupposes a detailed critique of contemporary American society, particularly as it relates to the issue of ecology. This critique was omitted from this volume for reasons of space; I hope it will appear elsewhere before too long. In the meantime I want to summarize it briefly here, lest what I take to be the very practical thrust of my essay be blunted.

My critique begins with an examination of the dominant American economic value, recently revived and celebrated with great fervor by President Nixon—*competition.* It suggests that competition as a way of life must be replaced by *cooperation,* internationally, nationally, and personally. The critique then examines some shortcomings of the contemporary ecology movement, especially the tendency of some of its faddish proponents to refuse to think of the possibility, not to say the necessity, of a thoroughgoing restructuring of our way of life. In a word, cleaning up our beaches and recycling tin cans are good things to do, but they are not enough. The issue is not the beautification of America, but the survival of humanity. The critique next examines a number of "cop-outs" that various people have made, either consciously or unconsciously, in order to avoid coming to realistic terms with the ecological crisis: 1) unquestioned trust in "the American way of life" and "our system of government;" 2) unquestioned trust in technology as a way of solving any problem that might arise; 3) unquestioned trust in "nature," going "back to nature" away from political responsibilities, following the path of Thoreau to Walden Pond (either literally or with the help of drugs, etc.); and 4) unquestioned trust in "the politics of consciousness" as a way to achieve social, political, and economic change, naively sitting back and waiting for Charles Reich's "Consciousness III" to transform our society by its own spiritual momentum, neglecting in the meantime the entrenched, immobile power of present day institutions and the groups in power. As we proceed, the reader with eyes to see will continually sense signs of this kind of implicit critique of our society.

The reader who would like to explore from a more substantive theological perspective some of the themes I touch on is encouraged to consult my study *Brother Earth: Nature, God, and Ecology in a Time of Crisis*.[2] This book seeks to view the contemporary ecological crisis in a broad historical context and then to offer a theological response, drawing on classical Christian symbols. I affirm what I said in *Brother Earth*; its underlying viewpoint is also reflected throughout the following pages. But the sense of urgency that I felt even then was purposely muted in that book, in order to provide what I hope was a balanced, in-depth theological analysis of and response to our present situation. Here, however, in keeping with the accent of practical theology, I am giving my intuitions and feelings much more room.

2. H. Paul Santmire, *op. cit.* (New York: Thomas Nelson, 1970).

My thoughts for this essay were first brought together in three lectures delivered at Nebraska Wesleyan University in the spring of 1971. I especially wish to thank the students there who gave me such an instructively critical hearing. I also want to thank several persons who read this essay, at various stages, and supplied helpful comments: Susan Andrews, Norman J. Faramelli, Scott I. Paradise, Gary C. Santmire, and Harold C. Santmire. It will be clear from the personal tone of what follows, however, that I alone am responsible for the contents and style, notwithstanding the good advice I have received. My deepest appreciation is for the understanding and support I continue to receive, both in times of joy and in times of fear, from my wife Laurel. This essay is dedicated in hope to our two children, Heather and Matthew. *In hope*—that the ecstasy of faith will help us all to avoid the ecological catastrophe now looming before us, and inspire us all to seek a new world of natural vitality and human justice, not only for our own benefit but for the sake of children everywhere.

H. P. S.

Chapter One

Love on
Spaceship Earth

"The most rational way of considering the whole human race today," writes Barbara Ward, "is to see it as the ship's crew of a single spaceship on which all of us, with a remarkable combination of security and vulnerability, are making our pilgrimage through infinity." An increasing number of ecologists, economists, philosophers, and theologians are adopting the image of "Spaceship Earth" as a framework for their thinking about the survival of humanity in our time of ecological crisis. "Our planet is not much more than a capsule," Barbara Ward continues, "within which we have to live as human beings if we are to survive the vast space voyage upon which we have been engaged for hundreds of millenia—but without noticing our condition. We depend upon a little envelope of atmosphere for life itself. And both can be contaminated and destroyed."[1]

Although the image of Spaceship Earth has certain significant limitations, I think it can be a very helpful image around which to organize our thoughts as we seek to avoid ecological catastrophe. The crisis before us is so serious that nothing less than a restructuring of our entire way of life is required. We need a new "system" for organizing our

1. Barbara Ward, *Spaceship Earth* (New York: Columbia University Press, 1966), p. 15.

society. This does *not* mean that we must "turn to the Left" in any traditional sense. Actually, the ecological record of most communist and non-democratic socialist countries has been no better, and has sometimes been worse, than ours. The new system we need must be truly *new*. This is why I think that the image of Spaceship Earth is so relevant. It seems to be well suited for opening up new economic, political, and social horizons that will allow us to organize our life on this planet in such a way that humanity can survive. Rightly understood, it seems to be just the "model" we need. I want now to describe this model in some detail and then to consider "the valuational fuel" that I think the Spaceship must have if it is to function properly. That valuational fuel I will identify as a rather specific, holistic, and realistic concept of love.

SPACESHIP EARTH

A model such as Spaceship Earth is to be distinguished from a Utopia, although good models necessarily include Utopian elements. In this sense, a good model functions as the proverbial carrot out in front of us, drawing us constantly toward the social, economic, and political approximations of ultimate, Utopian ideals.[2] But, in the main, a model is not a Utopia. More precisely, a model is what appears to us to be a workable general system, a long-range plan, that we design as an overall goal to guide our daily decisions. Accordingly, a model has a tentative character; it is not a blueprint. As we proceed to implement it as much as possible from day to day, a model is meant to be worked over, revised, even radically transformed in light of new experiences and new knowledge and new perspectives. In Alvin Toffler's words, a model must be seen

2. For discussions of the uses and abuses of Utopian thought, see Frank E. Manuel, ed. *Utopias and Utopian Thought* (Boston: Houghton Mifflin, 1966). The theological importance of Utopias is reviewed in this volume by Paul Tillich, "Critique and Justification of Utopias," pp. 296–309.

not as a static library of images, but as a living entity, tightly charged with energy and activity. It is not a 'given' that we passively receive from the outside. Rather, it is something we actively construct and reconstruct from moment to moment. Restlessly scanning the outer world with our senses, probing for information relevant to our needs and desires, we engage in a constant process of rearrangement and updating.[3]

In the spirit of openness to radically new goals and styles of life, then, and with the awareness that we are free to change our images and conceptions whenever that is necessary, I am suggesting that we explore the contours of the model Spaceship Earth.

Practically speaking, to implement the spaceship model a number of steps must be taken. *First,* population growth must be stabilized, in America as elsewhere, and then probably reduced below its present level.[4] Within America, moreover, careful policy distinctions must be made. Minority groups, especially blacks, are suspicious that population control means a policy of curtailment, even abolition, of minority groups. They remember, for example, urban renewal, that highly rationalized liberal scheme for rebuilding our inner cities. By and large Dick Gregory was right; urban renewal was, as a matter of fact, "Negro removal." It did not benefit the groups it was designed to benefit. Many blacks hear similar overtones and undertones in the pleasant-sounding music being played by advocates of population control (almost all of whom in America are white and affluent). And undoubtedly there is at least some justice in the feeling of blacks at this point. America contains within its past a genocidal propensity, dramatically evident in our

3. Alvin Toffler, *Future Shock* (New York: Random House, 1970), p. 178.

4. For a succinct review of the population problem, see Rufus E. Miles, Jr., "Whose Baby is the Population Problem?", *Population Bulletin,* XXVI, 2 (April, 1970), published by the Population Reference Bureau, Inc., Washington, D.C.

near extermination of the American Indian, and less dramatically but no less relentlessly evident in our treatment of the American black, from lynchings in the South to police brutality in the North. American history is shaped to this very day by a certain genocidal mind-set.

Recently in Boston, for example, a white suburban girl ran away from home under conditions that looked like she was kidnapped. The whole of New England was aroused; TV reporters interviewed her family and the police. The National Guard searched for her. It was first page news in most of the papers. In contrast, a short time before, a black girl disappeared from her home. Her mother could scarcely make the police take notice! Even when the girl managed to call home from the place to which she had been abducted, authorities took little notice. To the desperate mother they said, "She's a runaway." This actual kidnapping of the black girl was virtually unreported by the media. As it turned out, the white girl returned home, followed by TV cameras. The black girl was found dead in an empty room. This coincidence of events reflects a general genocidal mentality in our society—the assumption that a white life is worth more than a black life—a mentality that is also characteristic of at least some of our boys in Vietnam, who believe, and are willing to say so, that a "gook" is only worth a tenth or less of what any American is worth. So, while direct genocide of minority groups in this country seems unlikely, we must be sensitive to less visible attitudes that nevertheless point in the same direction.

In this connection Paul Ehrlich points out forcefully that the real population problem is rooted in the milieu of the affluent majority. Most babies are born to their families; and they consume and pollute far more than the minority groups, who are usually poor. Hence Ehrlich's conclusion is undoubtedly right; or at least the burden of proof is squarely on the shoulders of anyone who would deny his suggestion:

The best way to avoid any hint of genocide is to control the population of the dominant group. If this means an increase in the proportion of dark-skinned people in our society, so what? If blacks and whites cannot learn to enjoy their differences instead of using them as a basis of hatred, there will not be a world worth living in. If they do learn to live together with mutual cultural enrichment, then the exact mix of colors will be of little consequence.[5]

This is not somehow to suggest that members of minority groups should be denied access to birth control clinics, refused adequate education about population problems, and so on. It is simply to underline a point of emphasis: when, *if* it is necessary to do so, some kind of coercive population control measures must be introduced,[6] they should be directed first and foremost at the affluent white majority.

Secondly, material-consuming economic growth must also be radically reduced. A spaceship economy will be built on the premise that the good life requires only the production of goods that satisfy basic human needs, quantitatively and qualitatively.[7] The goal for food consumption, for example,

5. Paul Ehrlich and Richard L. Harriman, *How to Be a Survivor* (New York: Ballantine Books, 1971), p. 23. For another important perspective on this problem, see the statement by six poor black women, "Black Sisters," in *Masculine/Feminine: Readings in Sexual Mythology and the Liberation of Women,* eds., Betty and Theodore Roszak (New York: Harper and Row, 1969), pp. 212f.

6. The very mention of coercive measures to control population makes me very uneasy. This is an infinitely complex problem that has yet to be sufficiently analyzed by natural scientists and ethicists. For an introduction to the problem by one who will allow for coercive measures, see Ehrlich and Harriman, *op. cit.,* chap. III. See also the unpublished paper by Arthur J. Dyck, "Population Policies and Ethical Acceptability," Harvard Divinity School, June 18, 1970.

7. Kenneth E. Boulding, "The Economics of the Coming Spaceship Earth," in *Beyond Economics* (Ann Arbor: The University of Michigan Press, 1968), pp. 275–287; Herman E. Daly, "Toward a Stationary-State Economy," in *The Patient Earth,* eds., John Harte and Robert H. Socolow (New York: Holt, Rinehart and Winston, 1971); I. Alan Wagar, "Growth versus Quality of Life," *Science,* CLXVIII (June 5, 1970), pp. 1179–1184; Richard M. Koff, "An End to All This," *Playboy,* XVIII, 7 (July, 1971), pp. 112ff; Ezra J. Mishan, *The Costs of Economic Growth* (New York: Praeger, 1967).

will be nourishment for a minimal but balanced diet, and an occasional feast. The general rule for possessions will be simplicity and restraint. The age of the omnipresent gadget, from the air conditioner to the snowmobile, will have come to an end. Persons will recognize that an ever-increasing material growth is indeed the mark of the cancer cell, and that that kind of growth as a matter of course produces cancerous effects in the body politic.

Third, a heavy emphasis will be placed on recycling, since the Spaceship has a finite package of resources on board. Virtually everything that is used must be scrupulously re-used, by institutions as well as by individuals. *Fourth,* pollution obviously will be thoroughly reduced, and also strictly controlled where it is not totally removed. This will be brought about by a massive recycling program, on the one hand, and a program of mandatory pollution control (the costs of which will be carried by the polluters), on the other.[8] *Fifth,* competition as an institutional pattern of life will be demythologized. With so many passengers on such a fragile little ship, the passengers will have to find a moral alternative to fratricide, in the business world and in international politics, as well as in interpersonal relations. Self-limitation and a spirit of cooperation, by individuals, groups, and nations will be the order of the day. Perhaps in this respect the cultures of the East, in which competition and domination and compulsive material consumption have not been dominating motifs, will be able to help us to reshape our institutions.[9]

These five characteristics of the Spaceship model—a stable population; a non-growth, dynamic equilibrium economy;

8. Cf. Marshall I. Goldman, "The Costs of Fighting Pollution," *Current History,* (August 1970).

9. As one specific example, see E. F. Schumacher, "Buddhist Economics," *Resurgence,* I, 2 (January/February 1968). More generally, see Alan W. Watts, *Nature, Man and Woman* (New York: Random House, 1950).

massive recycling; total pollution control; and a constantly declining rate of fratricide—are matters of *survival*.

But mere survival is not enough. Anyone who has caught a glimpse of the biblical vision, or indeed anyone who has profoundly reflected on what it means to be human, will want the Spaceship to be more, much more, than a vehicle for survival. So, *sixth,* the Spaceship will be a place where all may enhance the quality of their lives. The ever growing national product in America will no longer be gross, but beautiful. Esthetic, scientific, philosophical, personal, and religious growth will be taken for granted. On the Spaceship, moreover, we will see a new, more sensitive land-use policy, for the public's sake directly, and also for the sake of insuring the longevity of our oxygen cycle. We will see an end to urban sprawl. Instead, many persons will live in densely populated, judiciously located clusters served by computerized mass transit systems; this will allow for broad sweeps of wilderness and cultivated land. The Spaceship will, in this respect, much more resemble an organism than a machine. Wild nature and cultivated nature will be preserved and enhanced; they will not be bulldozed away by fabricated nature. Even more, the wilderness and the agronomic elements of man's world will spill over into, and help to enliven, urban life, the primary home of fabricated nature. Cities and buildings and machines will be designed not merely functionally, but also organically, to call forth the pulse of wild and cultivated nature whenever they are touched and seen. There will also be little patches of wild nature and cultivated nature here and there in cities to remind us of the infinite universe outside the city limits.

The concentration of population in urban centers will also be an occasion for the pregnant kind of cultural life that has always been associated with the city at its best. The arts will flourish for citizens of all ages and places in society. At the same time, moreover, although there will be a certain degree of planned urban crowding, this will not mean the exclusion of cultural diversity and individual particularity. To be vital, any ecosystem requires diversity, and this the Spaceship will have in abundance, culturally as well as environmentally. The Spaceship will be rich with neighborhoods, each with its own characteristic flavor to lend to the whole.[10]

This cultural diversity, mirroring environmental variety, will in turn be reflected in the political institutions of the Spaceship. Although some kind of world government will certainly be required, it will *not* be a rigidly centralized government. Rather it will function more after the analogy of the plant; it will be multidirected. It will be representative and participatory. Although a totalitarian Spaceship is conceivable, there will be built-in safeguards to prevent a totally cephalized, heteronomous government. A vastly improved communications system, facilitated by thousands of computers, will help to insure a world community that will be responsive to the needs of all nations, all groups, and all individuals.[11]

Even more, *seventh*—and for some Americans this is the hardest thing to comprehend, though in biblical perspective it is absolutely essential—the Spaceship will be a place of social justice. Conceivably, by *de facto* or *de jure* means, a wealthy elite could dominate the Spaceship, Brave New World style, providing various forms of highly refined drugs to keep the majority happy with their hungry, dull, and suffering condition. But this alternative will be ruled out of court in the name of social justice.

The rich will therefore have to give up some of their

10. Cf. Daniel Callahan, "Self-Identity in an Urban Society," *Theology Today,* April, 1967.

11. For one significant treatment of the problem of world government, see the aforementioned work by Richard Falk, *Our Endangered Planet.* For a summary treatment of this and related issues, see Richard J. Niebanck, *World Community: Challenge and Opportunity,* published by the Board of Social Ministry, Lutheran Church in America, 231 Madison Avenue, New York, New York.

riches. They will have to recognize willingly, or else be forced to recognize, what should be a truism, that human rights take precedence over property rights. The trickle-down theory of getting wealth to the poor, letting the rich get richer, simply will not work anymore (if it ever did) in a spaceship economy, where, by definition, there is a limit to the accumulation of wealth, since the economy is not a constant growth economy. In a spaceship economy, the only way the rich would be able to get richer would be to steal from the poor; and that of course will be blocked. The rich will be required, by the development of new and creative economic institutions, to share some of their wealth with the remaining two-thirds of the people on the planet.[12] This will be required, both by law and by social pressure, since it will be taken for granted that there is only so much wealth to go around. Hence the only way the poor will ever get out of their plight will be by sharing in some kind of thoroughgoing redistribution of wealth. Individually, there will accordingly have to be an upper limit on incomes as well as a lower level, beneath which no one will be allowed to sink. And this redistribution of wealth will effect institutional fortunes too. Our churches and synagogues, for example, will have to begin redistributing their wealth. They before all others, of course! A recent study estimated that the total wealth of religious groups in this country is about 160 billion dollars, a figure higher than the combined assets of AT&T and the five largest oil companies.[13]

Internationally speaking, the well-fed American giant will have to reduce, along with other affluent European nations and Japan. Americans in particular will have to tone down

12. Some of the complexities of a planetary undertaking such as this are discussed by Thomas E. Weisskopf in his paper "Capitalism, Underdevelopment and the Future of Poor Countries," in J. N. Bhagwati, ed., *Economics and World Order* (New York: Macmillan Company, 1971).

13. Reported in *American Report,* October 9, 1970 (published by Clergy and Laymen Concerned about Vietnam, New York).

their voracious appetites for gadgets and hedonistic comforts such as large automobiles, sprawling one-family heated homes, air-conditioners, television sets, snowmobiles, *and* all the resource-consuming "gadgets" of modern warfare. All affluent Americans will have to learn *to consume less and enjoy it more,* for the sake of the rest of the passengers on the Spaceship and, ultimately, for the sake of their own survival. Denis Goulet has suggested, for the prosperous, "voluntary austerity" has come to be a necessary art.[14]

In such ways our present system will give way to the good Spaceship Earth. A profound spirit of restraint, sharing, and cooperation will be possible, like the promise of a fresh spring dew. The dearest freshness deep down things will begin to stir itself and to rise to the surface all over the globe.

Is all this preposterous? Is all this a deluded, Utopian dream? Has it any conceivable relationship to the "real world" in which we live? Well, the good Spaceship Earth as I have depicted it is a *goal,* a goal that we must work to achieve. And in that sense it is Utopian. But to say categorically that the good Spaceship Earth is—to use those venerable, mystifying, magic American words—"not practical" and to opt, whether implicitly or explicitly, for business as usual; to write off Spaceship Earth as a goal and, indeed, as a goal that we must attain with utmost haste, is to assume the classical stance of the much maligned ostrich, with his head in the sand.

I wonder, in other words, who is really in touch with reality and who is deluded, the proponent of Spaceship Earth or the proponent of the present order. *When, tutored by scores of responsible scientists, one sees the blood-dimmed tide, what other alternative is there but to opt for the dynamic equilibrium of a Spaceship Earth, for the sake of human survival? When, tutored by the biblical prophets and*

14. Denis A. Goulet, "Voluntary Austerity: the Necessary Art," *Christian Century,* June 3, 1966.

the teaching of Jesus, one sees the dearest freshness deep down things, what other alternative is there but to opt for the good quality and social justice of a Spaceship Earth, for the sake of man's humanity? What is human life without survival! And what is human survival without justice! Implementation of the Spaceship model I take to be an unavoidable necessity.

VALUATIONAL FUEL FOR THE SPACESHIP

But the Spaceship model by itself is not enough. Clearly we do need a model such as this for our survival's sake and for our humanity's sake. That is to say, we need a new social structure that will allow us to put an end to competition, domination, and excessive material consumption. The old "system" must be changed. The new model must be implemented. In other words, the "politics of consciousness" is not the quintessential reality;[15] we must change institutions as well as consciousness. Even so, the politics of consciousness *is* essential. The politics of consciousness is the flesh and blood without which the skeleton would be meaningless. Or, to use another figure, the politics of consciousness is the valuational fuel of the social model. Without a new consciousness, a new model will never function. Values and structures are interdependent realities; both are essential. *Society is empowered by human values, as well as held together by organizational structures.* Hence, we need a moral alternative to the old values of competition, domination, and compulsive material consumption, as well as a moral alternative to our old structural models. Spaceship Earth will never be a reality and will never be sustained without the values appropriate to it (nor of course will the new values be a reality and be sustained without the new model).

This is a large order. We immediately encounter the

15. Cf. the contrasting view of Charles Reich, *The Greening of America* (New York: Random House, 1970).

problem of universality and particularity. If our values are general enough to be understood and accepted by everyone on the planet, they may well be so simple and so vague that they will be of little concrete help. That is the danger of eclecticism. On the other hand, if our values are particular enough to be intelligibly related to the concrete situation, as we experience it, our values may well end up being merely *our* values, the values of white affluent liberal Americans, for example, and not really relevant as far as the rest of the world is concerned. This is the danger of parochialism.

I propose to handle this complicated problem of the universality versus the particularity of values by a common sense, rule-of-thumb procedure. I propose that we begin where we are, with our particularity, but that we begin with the broadest possible expression of that particularity. This, I hope, will steer us between the twin pitfalls of eclecticism and parochialism. Concretely, my feeling is that we have much to learn, ecologically speaking, from three divergent trends of thought in the contemporary Western Christian scene: religious naturalism, black theology, and catholic ecumenism. More concretely, I have in mind the work of Norman O. Brown, James H. Cone, and Pierre Teilhard de Chardin.

The one universal value that I see energizing Spaceship Earth is *love*. To highlight love in this way, of course, is not a revolutionary procedure. The praises of love have been sung by countless poets, theologians, and common folk. But that is just the problem. To say that you are in favor of love as the central universal value for the new ecological era is not to say very much at all. The critical point is reached only when one seeks to say what one means by love. And it is precisely at this juncture that I find Brown, Cone, and Teilhard refreshing and full of insights—though at the same time, they are all self-consciously writing within the particular confines of the modern Western Christian tradition.

Brown highlights one possible aspect of love, *eros,* bodily love. James H. Cone highlights another possible aspect, *philia,* love as fighting for social justice, for one's oppressed brothers, love as what he calls "black power." Pierre Teilhard de Chardin highlights a third dimension of this universal value: love as *agape.* This, in view of its universal scope, we can properly refer to as catholic love (with a small "c").

NORMAN O. BROWN: LOVE AS EROS

To understand Norman O. Brown we must clearly understand his context. As he himself relates, until 1948 he "held the enlightenment view that man has a limitless capacity to perfect himself by manipulating his environment."[16] Reason and progress are the hallmarks of that perspective. By a process of education and governmental reform, such as the New Deal tried to initiate, society will move closer and closer to a state of enlightenment. In the years following the election of 1948, however, Brown became increasingly disillusioned with that progressive approach to society.

To update this story I think we can understand Brown best if we see his work against the background of what has been called the Corporate State, that complex network of business, labor, university, and government that is directed toward "progress," that is, when "progress" is understood as manipulating the environment for the sake of achieving an ever increasing level of production and consumption. In the Corporate State, as a rule, persons are concerned more with means towards ends than with the ends themselves. A kind of superficial rationality dominates, the rationality of the technician, the expert, the man who gets things done, who has the skills to manipulate the environment successfully but who is not generally inclined to raise questions about why he is doing what he is doing. In

16. Norman O. Brown, interview, *Psychology Today,* August, 1970, p. 43.

Freudian terms, such a man is totally dominated by the ego, even tyrannized by it; moments of passion and feeling (the id) or moments of intense moral concern (the superego) do not dominate his style of life. His goal is basically to catch the 7:20 a.m. train and to sell more "Ban Roll-On."

In this overall endeavor the technician himself is more and more subsumed existentially by the power of the machines he operates. Technology, not positive humane values, tends to govern his life with its own momentum; and his individuality, in one way or another, tends to be mechanized. He tends to become a faceless servant of the machine, with suppressed feelings and dreams, lacking any driving moral passion. Even his sex life tends to be mechanized; it becomes a task to be mastered by studying manuals; and it becomes a victory to achieve, as in the pages of *Playboy,* surrounded by the self-indulgent, affluent furnishings of the penthouse apartment.

Norman O. Brown develops a radical protest against this allegedly enlightened, but actually effete "civilization" in which so many Americans live today. In the name of Freud and Christianity, Brown cries out for depth instead of artificiality, passion instead of cool technological detachment, union of mankind instead of fragmentation into countless isolated, competitive individuals. He calls for a rebirth of *eros.* This new "erotic sense of reality," he hopes, will lead us away from the lifeless, heartless, superficial rationality of technological society. At the same time, he also hopes, it will put an end to the habit of fratricide, which he sees as a characteristic of competitive industrial society.

Brown thus stands radically opposed to the Puritan Ethic, that compulsive American approach to work, activity, technological expertise, and the Gross National Product. For him, authentic humanity means *being* rather than acting, particularly being in a fleshly, bodily mode. "Doing nothing," Brown writes paradoxically, "if rightly understood is the supreme action."[17] That is to say, withdraw from your compulsive business, grades, quest for success, and all the rest, sink into the vitalities of your own body, feel the pulse of your unconscious, float on the fecund earth as a lily pad floats on a pond. Find what it means just to be, by yourself, in yourself.

Brown also stands over against major trends in our society insofar as he highlights the unconscious, not the ego or the superego, not the expertise or the social action, as the key to authentic human life. To *be,* for Brown, means to sink into the id, into the world of unconscious, undefined passion. And at that level, he believes, we are all one, united together in a single body, mystically:

> The unconscious is . . . that immortal sea which brought us hither; intimations of which are given in moments of 'oceanic feeling': one sea of energy or instinct; embracing all mankind, without distinction of race, language, or culture; and embracing all the generations of Adam, past, present, and future, in one phylogenetic heritage; in one mystical or symbolical body.[18]

With this emphasis on being in the flesh and sinking into the unconscious, Brown also paints a picture of a unified relationship with the whole material world. Nature is thereby eroticized. It is no longer that *thing* out there, which I transcend, and which I may manipulate as I see fit. Nature is, as it were, my greater body.[19] One participates mystically in nature, rather than manipulating it and exploiting it. One has a love affair with every tree. Every meal is holy communion.

It may be surprising to some, but Brown supports his aphoristic argument by frequent references to the classical

17. Norman O. Brown, *Love's Body* (New York: Random House, 1966), p. 105.

18. *Ibid.,* pp. 88f.

19. *Ibid.,* pp. 226f.

Christian tradition, and especially to the emphasis that tradition places on the incarnation and the resurrection of the body. Interestingly, too, Brown is very much impressed, not to say captivated, by the thought and life of Martin Luther. He finds Luther's earthiness and his concern for bodily vitalities impressive. Brown also applauds Luther's realistic, albeit paradoxical, approach to the devil and the end of the world. Above all, Brown celebrates Luther's emphasis on justification by faith and not by works.[20] Among the biblical writers Brown refers most frequently to St. Paul, and particularly to Paul's view that all men are one in Adam and made new in the mystical body of the risen Christ.

Brown surely can be faulted at several points. In a sense the only real love he knows is *eros*, the quest for being and union and participation in the immediate moment. This leads him to maintain that human history is going nowhere and that human individuality—which he identifies with the ego —is best if it is abolished. Similarly, and ironically, Brown's emphasis on *eros* tends to lead him away from concrete eroticism! For him, his much quoted phrase, "polymorphous perversity," has more to do with the imagination and poetry than with physical eroticism as such. He rejects, likewise, sexual differentiation as a sign of the fall. In this respect his world is quite different from the biblical world he likes to refer to, especially as that world comes to expression in the Song of Songs, the delightful biblical love poem of joyous sex. Finally, Brown urges a flight from politics, again constructing a world radically different from the biblical world. "The next generation," he explains, "needs to be told that the real fight is not the political fight, but to put an end to politics. From politics to metapolitics."[21]

20. Brown's most extended treatment of Luther is to be found in *Life Against Death: The Psychoanalytic Meaning of History* (New York: Vintage Books, 1959), chap. XIV.
21. *Ibid.,* pp. 41, 47, 50, 85–86, 196, 226. And Brown, "Reply to Marcuse," *Commentary,* XLIII, 3 (March 1967), pp. 46, 83.

So this great champion of human unity does not concretely champion union between the sexes and union between groups and nations! The concrete world of sex and politics tends to become a shadow world in Brown's thought. The real world seems to become the ineffable nothingness of the undifferentiated unconscious.[22] Related to this, one misses in Brown's work any consistent emphasis on celebration and festivity and joy. He is so serious! But as Freud himself is said to have remarked once, when someone asked him about the psychological significance of his cigar, "Sometimes a cigar is just a smoke." Likewise, sometimes skiing, for example, is just a joyous trip downhill, in exhilarating air, and not necessarily a phallus plunging into mother earth, driven by a death wish, returning to the womb. Sometimes skiing is just for fun! In contrast, generally, the result of Brown's work is a deep morass of unconscious seriousness.

These are some of the most noticeable flaws in Brown's vision. But they should not blind us to the real contribution he has made to our world, a world that so often is hypercompetitive, compulsively busy, exploitatively oriented, superficially rational, and fratricidally fragmented. Brown has shown us a compelling vision of being, union, and vitality. And this is a vision that the coming Spaceship Earth will definitely need: vibrant, vital wholeness. Life on the Spaceship will be less than human if it is dominated by the machine and its mentality, as technologically speaking it might well be. Our Spaceship must be organically oriented and integrated. It will require a rebirth of *eros*, of the body.

JAMES H. CONE: LOVE AS PHILIA

When we turn to the thought of James H. Cone, we enter an entirely different kind of milieu. Though Cone would not take issue with all of what Brown says, his characteristic

22. Cf. Herbert Marcuse, "Love Mystified: A Critique of Norman O. Brown," *Commentary*, XLIII, 3 (March 1967), p. 73.

interests lie elsewhere, in the political arena. Note the title of his best known work, *Black Theology and Black Power.*[23] In Cone's thought we meet the universal value of love not so much as *eros,* but much more as *philia.* This is love for the brother, for the oppressed members of the family of man. Accordingly, the biblical theme in the background is no longer predominantly the unity of mankind in Adam and in Christ. Rather, it is mainly the theme of God's care for the poor, as in Jesus' parable of the Good Samaritan. Cone calls for a rebirth of *philia,* biblically understood.

Obviously, the context within which Cone is best understood is not that of the Corporate State as such, but—closely related to it—white racism. This is not the place to review this much discussed topic. In brief, the term refers to the systematic discrimination and persecution of non-white peoples around the world by powerful, affluent whites, a discrimination and a persecution that frequently is institutionalized and thereby not the "fault" of any one individual.

James Cone would say to Norman Brown: all this being, and all this striving for reunion with the unconscious of mankind that makes us all one, and all this quest for vitality, means nothing if the people and the institutions embodying white racism remain unchanged. Indeed, Cone might continue, the black man has long known how to be in his body, how to be united with his brother by soul force, and how to participate in the rhythms of nature. But what is all this when he is dragged from his home and beaten, and the perpetrators go free!? What is *eros* without *philia?* What is bodily vitality without social justice?

The heart of Cone's thought is the identification of the message and work of Jesus with the revolutionary forces behind the movement of black liberation. Cone's Jesus is

23. James H. Cone, *Black Theology and Black Power* (New York: Seabury, 1969). Cone has developed his perspective more systematically in his essay, *A Black Theology of Liberation* (Philadelphia: J. B. Lippincott, 1970).

the one who separates the sheep and the goats on the Last Day, according to whether they gave food to the hungry and water to the thirsty; the Jesus who drove the money changers from the temple with a whip; the Jesus who said that it is easier for a camel to go through the eye of a needle than for a rich man to enter the Kingdom of God; the Jesus who cast out demons; the Jesus who came to set free those who are oppressed. For Cone, "Jesus's work is essentially one of liberation." "In Christ," Cone explains, "God enters human affairs and takes sides with the oppressed." Concretely, this means that Christ is opposed to white racism as a power of the devil. At the same time Christ's mission is to heal the wounds of self-hatred that whites have inflicted on blacks.[24] In this sense, Cone points out, Christianity is not alien to Black Power; it *is* Black Power. The Church, accordingly, is properly thought of not primarily as a place where individuals gather at 11 a.m. on Sundays to worship with Word and Sacrament, but as a revolutionary community: "The Church is that people called into being by the power and love of God to share in his revolutionary activity for the liberation of man."[25] The Church is the Church, in one word, when it truly knows blackness.

This is not to say that Cone excludes whites from the Church. On the contrary, he expressly includes "blackmen in white skins." In other words, blackness for Cone is fundamentally a *socio-political category,* not a physiological category. As he remarks, "Being black in America has very little to do with skin color. To be black means that your heart, your mind, and your body are where the dispossessed are."[26]

Such a vision of blackness, of love as *philia,* must shape the life of the coming Spaceship Earth. The good Spaceship

24. Cone, *Black Theology and Black Power,* pp. 35f., 40, 62.
25. *Ibid.,* pp. 38, 63.
26. *Ibid.,* pp. 3, 151. In *A Black Theology of Liberation* Cone defines blackness not only as a socio-political concept, but also an ontological term.

Earth can only be called good if it is energized by a deep passion for social justice, as we have already had occasion to observe. A Spaceship dominated by racism would not be worth the trouble of building and maintaining. All the population and pollution control, and all the recycling in the word, would be for naught without a modicum of institutionalized brotherhood. Not brotherhood as a slogan, I hasten to add, but brotherhood as a social reality, reenforced by social institutions. Indeed, it could be that *the* place to begin "paying reparations to nature," maybe *the* place to focus the attention and the work of any ecology movement, is the rat infested black ghetto. Renewal of the earth would be a travesty without liberation of the wretched of the earth.

If we need a Norman O. Brown to teach us how to resurrect the body and the natural order, we also need a James H. Cone to teach us how to transform the social order. We need a James H. Cone, too, to correct some one-sided elements in Brown's eroticism. Brown's rejection of politics in favor of metapolitics is understandable in his own terms, but it surely cannot be allowed to stand unchallenged. For surely the vitalities of the body can only really flourish fully in a context of social justice. What, after all, is the beauty of the body of a young American boy if it is blown to pieces in a ghetto rebellion? What, after all, is the beauty of a Vietnamese mother nursing her child, if she is thrown into a ditch and shot? *Eros* to be *eros,* and not just another name for death, needs *philia.* And vice versa to be sure. Justice can never be merely quantitative, merely a mechanistic distribution of goods. Justice always wants to be qualitative as well, to offer a sense of vitality and joy, along with the package of food and clothing. With this point, I am sure, James H. Cone would agree. He would not hesitate to say that black is beautiful. He would not hesitate to celebrate the black body and the vitality of black music and the deep sense of psychological unity that black people feel.

PIERRE TEILHARD DE CHARDIN: LOVE AS AGAPE

But our vision of love is not yet complete. If we need a Norman O. Brown to call us to immersion in bodily vitalities, and if we need a James H. Cone to call us to immersion in the work of human liberation, we also need a Pierre Teilhard de Chardin to call us to immersion in the process of universal reconciliation. Brown has already taken us in this direction, with his emphasis on the unity of mankind. But, as we saw, Brown holds that history is going nowhere. Brown has little hope for a new state of things. For him, "everything remains always the same."[27] Without negating the eroticism, Cone has shown us a way beyond this erotic nihilism in Brown's thought. Yet Cone has not explicitly shown us the way beyond the day of political liberation. This is understandable, since the reality of oppression hangs so heavily over Cone's thought.

Still, there *is* an era beyond the revolution. And that is what Teilhard helps us to see. This is the universal era of reconciliation, the era of *agape*. This is the goal toward which history is moving, penultimately and ultimately. We need this kind of catholic value for our Spaceship Earth, lest life be thought to come to nothing, to be swallowed up by death, and hence finally to be meaningless, which is the way Brown's thought would lead us, were it taken alone; lest life be thought to reach its apex in the disjunctive, painful reality of revolution, which is the way Cone's thought might lead us, were it taken alone.[28]

27. Brown, "Reply to Marcuse," p. 83.
28. Because of his interest in the revolutionary politics of the present, Cone radically reduces his treatment of the coming future Kingdom of God. "Too much of this talk is not good for the revolution," he remarks (*A Black Theology of Liberation*, p. 249). This is an understandable overstatement. But it *is* an overstatement. If there is no ultimate victory of righteousness, the God who liberates men today is playing idle games with the oppressed; he is leading them on, only to let them fall over the brink. And that would mean—in Cone's terms—that, when all has been said and done, God is not black but white. A theology of liberation entails what I am calling a theology of reconciliation, or it is a sham theology.

This is not the place to describe Teilhard's vision in full.[29] But it will be important for us to identify some of its prominent themes. For Teilhard, the whole universe is going somewhere. It is an immense process of becoming, an infinite sea of genesis. Creation did not happen once upon a time, way back then. Creation is the underlying reality of this universe now. Divine creativity is the *milieu* of our cosmos, of our galaxy, of our planet, of our history. And the essence of that creativity is *agape,* self-giving love, reconciling love. God is continually pouring out his life to the cosmos, guiding it (on its own terms) to greater and greater intensifications of *agape.*

According to Teilhard, with the birth of man and human history, the universal process of evolution passed into a new phase. Evolution since then has mainly followed the route of culture and politics. But it remains evolution nevertheless. Gradually, through a painfully long history, man has filled the planet, developed systems of culture, and communicated among cultures. In this regard, Teilhard believes, man's technology is a tool for his continuing evolution. Technology, especially mass communications, serves to bring the human race together, to forge new ties of unity between groups and nations. Hence Teilhard looked at the birth of the United Nations, for example, as an event of profound cosmic significance! Here was a start, he believed, however faltering, toward unification of the human race, reconciliation of those who oppose each other, in terms of peace and justice and freedom. The birth of the UN was for Teilhard a prefiguring of a new era of planetary solidarity, a new stage in the history of evolution.

For Teilhard, the whole history of evolution—through a highly complicated and extended process of "cosmic drift"— is aimed at the creation of an integrated world society on

29. For one astute study, see Robert Faricy, *Teilhard de Chardin's Theology of the Christian in the World* (New York: Sheed and Ward, 1967).

planet earth. This, he believed, is the underlying goal of the divine self-giving: to bring the whole family of man into one society of peace and justice. This world society, as Teilhard depicted it, will be a synthesis of the "best elements" of Democracy, Communism, and Fascism. It will embody the democratic sense of the rights of the person, the communist vision of the potentialities contained in matter, and the fascist ideal of an organized elite.[30] This world society is the penultimate goal of the divine *agape*. Beyond this, according to Teilhard, we can look forward to an ultimate Day of the final Omega Point, the transcendent Day of the final fulfillment of the whole cosmos in the immediate white heat of the presence of God himself. The Omega Point is thus the transcendent heavenly power of the divine *agape*. It draws all things to itself, reconciling them, unifying them, affirming them.

All this, for Teilhard, is to occur *with* the help of man's works of love, which are an expression of the universal process of reconciliation. The person who builds up the unified body of mankind is in fact, says Teilhard, a living extension of the creative power of God.[31] Unconsciously all men of good will collaborate in building the Kingdom of God.

For Teilhard, in contrast to Brown, the history of man, indeed of the whole cosmos, *is* going somewhere. There is a transcendent goal of fulfillment in which struggling humanity may hope, and after which it may model its life. There is, moreover, a personal center in the universe, God himself, and this center ultimately validates the being and the work of every individual. The individual is not lost in the collective in Teilhard's thought, as the individual tends to be in Brown's thought. As Teilhard states, "Our God . . . pushes to its fur-

30. Teilhard de Chardin, *Building the Earth*, n. tr. (Wilkes-Barre, Pa.: Dimension Books, 1965), p. 32.
31. Teilhard, *The Divine Milieu, n. tr.* (New York: Harper and Row, 1957), p. 62.

thest possible limit the differentiation among the creatures he concentrates within himself."[32] In a like manner, and again in contrast to Brown, Teilhard affirms the importance of human rationality. Of course, as far as Teilhard is concerned, if human rationality is to help build up the earth, it will have to be creative and imaginative. It will be rationality shaped by the self-giving love of God. Similarly, and once again over against the stance of Brown, Teilhard affirms the intrinsic humanity of the political process. The way to planetary unity for Teilhard is not by revoking politics, but by going through politics and transforming the whole political order.

With regard to the stance of James Cone, Teilhard shows us a way beyond the disjunctive politics of revolution. He shows us a unified planet whose citizens live in peace and justice. He shows us the possibility of reconciliation among all men. This is not to deny, as I indicated earlier, the need for a politics of liberation. It is rather to observe that, properly understood, the politics of liberation is complemented and fulfilled by the politics of reconciliation.

At the same time there are some jagged edges in Teilhard's thinking that need to be smoothed down. The first is a certain one-sided *spiritualism*. The second is a certain exaggerated *optimism*. In these respects Teilhard's thought needs to be corrected by Brown's and Cone's respectively.

Teilhard approaches matter as if it were merely the instrument or the stage for the birth and unification of spirit. In a letter he writes, "I do not attribute any definitive or absolute value to the varied constructions of nature. What I like about them is not their particular form, but their function, which is to build up mysteriously, first what can be divinized, and then, through the grace of Christ coming upon our endeavor, what is divine. . . ." "All reality," he says similarly in the *Divine Milieu*, "even material reality, around each

32. *Ibid.,* p. 116.

one of us, exists for our souls." The task of man, accordingly, is to ascend up the ladder of matter, "as a series of foot-holds."[33] Teilhard frequently thinks of this ascent in terms of conquest; man conquers the earth.

In itself, according to Teilhard, matter contains "a certain quantity of spiritual power." This is spiritual matter, so-called. One day, all of this spiritual matter will have passed *into the souls of men,* and at this point the world will be ready for the second coming of Christ.[34] With the Second Coming all "carnal matter" will be dissipated; it will fall back into nothingness, and the souls of men and Christ alone will remain united with God. This is the shape of Teilhard's one-sided spiritualism.[35]

This needs to be corrected, urgently, I should observe, because this brand of spiritualism reflects the thinking of a pre-Spaceship society. *The* ecological failure of industrial society has been its underlying tendency to approach the human body and the whole environment as a mere instrument, whose only purpose is to provide man with resources for so-called economic progress. That is the hallmark of the exploitative, manipulative industrial approach to nature.

In contrast, the view we will want to take, within the context of a Spaceship Earth, will be more biblical and more in line with the thought of Brown. True, evolution has a uni-linear aspect when seen in theological perspective. Man and his rationality, profoundly understood, in one sense *is* the high-est product of evolution. On the other hand, we will also main-tain, evolution has a multi-linear aspect as well. Every level of the evolutionary process has its own integrity, and its own value in the eyes of God. The human body, in particular, has its own integrity and its own rights for fulfillment. It is not merely the platform for the soul. In keeping with this, we

33. *Ibid.,* pp. 93, 56, 108.
34. *Ibid.,* pp. 109, 110.
35. See also the material cited in Santmire, *op. cit.,* p. 214, n. 2.

will want to say that man properly relates himself to nature with respect, delight, and wonder, that he relates to it as an end in itself, and not just manipulatively. To be human, in other words, is to be able to say "brother body" and "brother earth," as well as to say "what is man that Thou art mindful of him."[36]

Teilhard's exaggerated optimism also needs to be corrected. It is by no means certain that mankind will, as he suggests, inevitably move toward unification and the Omega Point. On the contrary, it is entirely conceivable that entrenched power groups may refuse to share their wealth, or that the affluent few may refuse to share their food with the starving millions, and that this will lead to another and final world war. Thermonuclear or chemical-biological war as a result of accident or madness is also conceivable. The human race may be deceased long before it is unified, and long before it approaches Point Omega. So our Spaceship Society must be defined with attention to power groups and individual self-assertion.

Here Teilhard can be corrected fruitfully from the side of James Cone. Following Tillich, Cone holds that power is an essential dimension of social organization. The world society of the good Spaceship Earth, therefore, must be structured to channel and to harmonize collective political power struggles and to check individual power struggles and individual acts of self-assertion or madness. On the Spaceship, in other words, power *will* be employed, and the institutions of society, from the most comprehensive to the smallest, will be so defined. But power will not be employed as an end in itself; rather, it will be employed creatively to provide a living space for *eros* and *agape*, for immersion in the vitalities of nature and for participation in the universal processes of reconciliation.

36. This paragraph summarizes several of the major points of my study *Brother Earth*, especially chapters IV, VI, and VII.

These are the new visions I think we must attend to. The model will be Spaceship Earth. The valuational energy will be the power of love, a love that is both holistic and realistic. This love will be *bodily*, it will be *black*, and it will be *catholic*. It will be variously experienced as *eros*, as *philia*, and as *agape*. But how do these new visions hold together?

Chapter Two

Our Pilgrimage
Through Infinity

To try to unite *eros, philia,* and *agape* appears to be a precarious undertaking. To bring together the thought of a Norman O. Brown, a James H. Cone, and a Pierre Teilhard de Chardin is apparently to create an unstable compound. That should be evident by now. Although these three thinkers certainly can be read—as I have read them—as complementing each other, they can also be taken as opposed to each other in several important respects, some of which we have already had occasion to notice.

I am convinced that these visions do hold together. One reason why they do is right at hand, although it is by no means evident for many people today. We have seen it with varying degrees of explicitness in the perspectives of Brown, Cone, and Teilhard. *The new visions hold together because ultimately, in reality, they are held together.*

At this point, we move from the relatively tangible dimension of talk about models and values to the relatively intangible dimension of talk about religious intuitions.[1] The

1. Insofar as we are now touching explicitly on the dimension of the ultimate (God), our language takes on a new kind of "charge." The factual kind of language describing the spaceship model, and the more personal kind of language describing the values of love, are now taken up into the intuitive religious language of "symbolic realism." For a discussion of the latter concept, see Robert Bellah, *Beyond Belief: Essays on Religion in a Post-Traditional World* (New York: Harper and Row, 1970), chap. XV.

spotlight thus far has been on the problematic ecological life of man in the center of the stage on planet Earth, and on new possibilities for human life, possibilities for survival and for a better quality of life and a higher level of social justice. Now we see the scope of the spotlight widening. Now, tutored still by Brown, Cone, and Teilhard, we will attempt to catch glimpses of a *real correspondence.* This is the correspondence between the envisioned world of Spaceship Earth, which is to be energized by the three forms of love, and *an enveloping universal process of divine creativity.*

In this context, therefore, we may appropriately see a deeper religious meaning in Barbara Ward's picture of mankind aboard a single Spaceship. To recall her words: *We are making our pilgrimage through Infinity.* In a word, we are embarked on a cosmic journey in the midst of Ultimate Reality. I will not argue that everyone must see this kind of greater religious vision in order for the model and the values we have been considering to make sense. But I will give testimony that I for one, when I think of Spaceship Earth and the power of love, find the mystical horizon now before us deeply satisfying, positively inspiring, and existentially indispensable.

Two remarks for the sake of orientation: First, none of our tutors takes us away from the concrete world in which we live. Each is concerned to identify the reality of God not in some eternal world far removed from our concrete experience, but right in the midst of that experience. The infinite process of divine creativity that we will be seeking to catch sight of will appear as *permeating* as well as enveloping the world of lived experience. *Eros, philia,* and *agape* will be seen as rooted in the *immediate* presence of God.

Second, each of our three tutors—in varying degrees and in different ways—relies on the "spectacles" of biblical faith in order to see mystically. Norman O. Brown draws inspiration from the fleshly theology of the Old Testament, the body mysticism of St. Paul, and the biblical theology of Martin Luther. James H. Cone speaks self-consciously from the perspective of the prophetic tradition of the Old Testament, and the New Testament (especially the Lukan) witness to the life of Jesus. Pierre Teilhard de Chardin depends heavily on the cosmic theology of Colossians and Ephesians. At the same time, however, the three do not present their religious intuitions with the same kind of intensity. Brown presupposes many theological themes, but he touches on most of them only in passing. Cone, even in his most systematic work, is reluctant to deal at length with any theological theme not directly related to black liberation. Teilhard, in contrast to both Brown and Cone, develops a highly explicit, comprehensive theology. In view of these varying degrees of theological explicitness in the works of our tutors, it seems most promising to be instructed, as I have indicated, by their particular religious apperceptions, but only in so far as we can see those apperceptions taking shape ourselves, through the spectacles of biblical faith.

For those who are so inclined, we may begin the process of "seeing through a glass darkly," peering into the mystical nimbus surrounding and permeating the world of Spaceship Earth, to try to catch a glimpse of that numinous depth of reality that gives unity and substance to the values of *eros, philia,* and *agape.* Right away we can see signs of a creative God who is living, who is holy, and who is gracious.

THE LIVING GOD

As the Living God, the Creator invigorates us and our cosmos by his vital Spirit. The life-giving divine Spirit, surging and flowing like deep ocean currents in the primordial depths of reality, gives our universe its being and its becoming.[2] So the account of creation in Genesis depicts God's

2. Much of the following material is treated at length in my study, *Brother Earth,* chaps. IV, VI, and VII.

110

Spirit as moving over the face of the primeval waters (Gen. 1:2). So the Psalmist speaks of the abundance of God's creative works: "When thou sendest forth thy Spirit, they are created; and thou renewest the face of the ground" (Ps. 104:30). The Spirit of God is the life-giving source and fountain of all things. Emphatically, this refers to the universe *at this very moment,* not to a world that was constructed once upon a time by some cosmic watchmaker, who has since withdrawn from his project. The Living God is no watchmaker; he is—if we use the term cautiously—the Life Force of all things. In this sense Luther refers to the world of nature as "the mask of God." The Living God is not alien to nature (as is the distant deity of popularized Greek philosophy). On the contrary, his majesty and glory *resemble* the majesty and the glory of the wonders of the natural world (cf. Ps. 29; Ro. 1: 20). Here we can be instructed by the oft-cited remark of the German Lutheran Pietist, Friedrich Oetinger, "corporality is the end of the ways of God." This is not to suggest that God somehow has a body, but much more profoundly and mystically that God's own being is a vibrant ocean of infinite vitality. It is also to suggest that God takes joy both in his own vitality and in the life he communicates to all his creatures, large and small (cf. Ps. 104:31).

This last point concerning God's rejoicing deserves emphasis. God does not rule the universe majestically, and nurture all his creatures with infinite care, simply because *man* is on the scene. Incredible as it may seem, what most major modern Western theologians have maintained is that the universe is solely a platform brought into being for the sake of God's history with *man.* All the millions of galaxies and the virtually infinite expanses of cosmic time are there for man's sake! Little man. Without denying this motif, I want to see it set in a much larger context, the context of the divine rejoicing. God rejoices in *all* his creative works, not just in the particular history of mankind. To employ Norman O. Brown's terms, God has an *erotic* sense for the whole of reality. God daily brings into being and sustains a world full of variety—colors, sizes, patterns, shapes, sounds, tastes, and so on—for the sake of his own pleasure. This, in all likelihood, is what the cadence of confessions in Genesis I means, in part: "And God saw that it was good."[3] God takes pleasure in all the creative works of his vital Spirit.

More particularly, God takes special delight in his special creature, man. God creates man "out of the dust"—out of the infinite epochs of cosmic space-time. God calls man forth, when the time is ripe, from the earth, and he continues to shape and nurture the life of man. Moreover, God creates man *in his image*. In the book of Genesis, interestingly, this phrase seems to refer most directly not to man's reason (as many theologians have maintained), but to man's *bodiliness*.[4] In the vitalities of his bodily existence, man reflects—he "images forth"—the life of God himself. This motif is taken for granted by Luther, I think, when he comments: "The fact that Adam and Eve walked about naked was their greatest adornment before God and all creatures." Accordingly, it is given to man to reflect God's erotic sense for the whole of reality. It is given to man by God to rejoice in man's own bodily vitalities and in the world of nature (cf. Ps. 104; Mt. 6: 29). This is the natural legacy of one created according to the image of the Living God. Man is called forth from the earth, every day, to live in *eros*.

THE HOLY GOD

As the Holy God, the Creator permeates the affairs of men by his righteous power. He establishes political channels and structures to promote and to insure a righteous life for his special creature, man. In this sense God continually creates

3. See Santmire, *op. cit.,* p. 209, note 4.
4. *Ibid.,* p. 222, note 6.

man to be a political animal, to live *in community* under the aegis of justice. So the writer of the Book of Revelation as a matter of course depicts the fulfillment of man's life as a time of peace and justice in the city of God (Rev. 21:1f.). Likewise, the writer of II Peter looks forward not only to a new heavens and a new earth (this has been emphasized by the pastoral romantics in the Christian tradition); he looks forward to "a new heavens and a new earth *in which righteousness dwells*" (II Peter 3:13). A life of peace with justice in community—that is the divinely established destiny of mankind. That is the will of the Holy God for his special creature, man.

Clearly, the divine righteousness is not some abstract quality or merely an attribute of an isolated deity. Like the vitality of the divine Spirit, the righteousness of the divine power is to be found in the midst of human experience, in this case in the midst of human politics. This is at least part of the meaning of Jesus' parabolic, prophetic ride into the midst of Jerusalem, where he cleansed the temple (cf. Mt. 21:1-13). Jesus can be appropriately interpreted at this point as radiating the righteous power of God. For like his life, God's righteousness is no distant eternal quality. It is his power for justice, active throughout the scope of human history. To speak in the vernacular, God is involved in politics. By his righteous power he is at work wherever men live, creating a life for man in a community that is full of justice. So the prophet Amos sees God not only working for justice in the history of the nation Israel, but also in the history of other nations (Amos 1, 2). God's active righteous power is everywhere shaping human politics creatively, so that righteousness may roll continually down, like an everlasting stream. (Amos 6:24).

The overall exercise of God's righteous power, the creative pressure for justice he exerts on the affairs of men everywhere, takes a special form in relation to contexts of radical injustice, particularly with regard to the history of oppressed peoples. As James Cone has so forcefully argued, the righteousness of God takes the form of *liberation* of oppressed peoples as it bears upon their affairs. This theme can be seen paradigmatically in the story of the Exodus, and with singular power in the Lukan picture of Jesus as the one who comes "to set at liberty those who are oppressed" (Luke 4:18). Even from the lips of "gentle Mary" we hear these frequently sung but infrequently understood words concerning God:

> He has put down the mighty from their thrones, and exalted those of low degree; he has filled the hungry with good things, and the rich he has sent empty away. (Lk. 1:52f.)

As the Holy God, the Creator exercises his righteous power everywhere in the history of man, and concretely through the institutions of man. At the same time, God's activity comes to a special focus on the life of the oppressed in the world: the Jews in Russia; the peasants in Vietnam; the malnourished and poverty-stricken masses in Latin America, Asia, and Africa; the blacks, the Indians, the Puerto Ricans, the chicanos, and the poor Appalachian whites in America. In this sense, God is on *their* side. He attends first and foremost to their needs, leaving the ninety-nine righteous (affluent) to seek out the one who is lost (poor).

Accordingly, God speaks to men and women everywhere in their consciences to persuade them and to inspire them to image-forth his righteous power. He calls upon all persons to become involved in the creative processes of politics and particularly in the struggle for the liberation of oppressed peoples. God calls all mankind to a life of *philia*. So, characteristic of biblical thinking generally, Jesus does ask his followers to take note of the glories of the lilies in nature, but he quickly moves to the further point that his disciples should seek *first* the Kingdom of God and his righteousness (Mt. 6:33). This is the historical legacy of the creature, man, who is created according to the image of the Holy God. Man is called forth from the earth, every day, to live in *philia,* as well as in *eros.*

THE GRACIOUS GOD

As the Gracious God, the Creator is the one who blesses all men and women with life and liberty, and who brings us all together into the family of man through his self-giving compassion, *agape.* Moreover, as we saw in the case of God's vital Spirit and his righteous power, God's grace is no abstract, timeless quality or attribute. The image refers to all his activity throughout the universe, as he envelops and permeates it. This is stated in a striking way by the Psalmist in his liturgy of grace, Psalm 136. He celebrates God's grace[5] in the wonders and blessings of nature (vv. 4-9), in his history with the oppressed people Israel (vv. 10-24), and in his universal gift of food "to all flesh" (v. 25). This is the same God whom the writer of I John identifies as *agape* (I Jn. 4:8).

But God's self-giving compassion is not only his *agape* in this present world, as he seeks to bless all peoples with life and liberty. It is also his *promise* for all things and all peoples: his promise for cosmic and historical fulfillment. All God's actions in nature and in history, his works of life-giving and his works of righteousness, are shaped not only as ends in themselves, but also as pilgrim steps along the way. The universe is a cosmic and historical symphony of divine life and righteousness, shaped along the way by the grace of God, proceeding to a glorious climax of consummated *agape.* God is drawing all things and all peoples forward, everywhere at all times, toward the mysterious Day of his new

5. I am translating the Hebrew *hsd* here by the word grace, rather than by the expression used by the Revised Standard Version, "steadfast love." Properly interpreted, "grace" is a much better translation.

heavens and new earth, toward the perfected City of God. In the words of Colossians, so cherished by Teilhard de Chardin, God is at work in all things, from the beginning to the very end, "to reconcile to himself all things" (Col. 1:20). On that final Day, according to St. Paul, God will be all in all (I Cor. 15:28). That is the transcendent goal toward which all things and all men are moving every day, the final banquet of divine grace.

With this ultimate goal in view, it becomes clear that the penultimate goal of God is greater and greater unity within the family of man in every period. God is at work at all times to reverse the fragmentation in his human family, a fragmentation symbolized by the story of the Tower of Babel. By his *agape,* God is working at this very moment to set the solitary in families, (Ps. 68.6) to see the brethren dwell in unity (Ps. 133:1), and to bring the many nations together in his peace (Zech. 2:11). Things are moving toward greater and more righteous expressions of human solidarity and community in this world. These expressions of community are variegated prefigurations of the ultimate Day of unity and fulfillment.[6]

It must be emphasized, however, that the divine way of unity is frequently if not always the way of pain and suffering, given the conditions of a distorted human world. So Israel's mission among the nations, according to Isaiah, is to be for God's sake the "suffering servant." Likewise, according to St. Paul (Phil. 2:5), Jesus is given by God a mission of self-sacrifice. This is to reveal the depths of the Divine *agape.* The way of unity for the family of man is invariably the way of self-giving, Divine compassion for the sake of the estranged and the oppressed. God suffers with (*cum-*

6. We touch here on a complicated problem: is there *progress* in human history? This question requires such an intricate answer that I propose to leave it unanswered here, except to say: there *is* a certain progress in human history; but with every advance there is a corresponding advance in the human potential for doing evil.

passio) his fragmented human family so that its members may find fulness of life by coming together. The writer of Colossians even extends this motif to the entire cosmos. When he says that God reconciles all things to himself in Christ, he notes that in this way God makes peace "by the blood of the cross" (Col. 1: 20).

The role of man in this context, accordingly, is to image-forth the grace of God, to imitate the *agape* of God. The proper stance for man is to be ever prepared to give of himself for the sake of blessing and liberating others. The authentic walk of man is to proceed so that the forsaken may find families, so that the brothers and the sisters may dwell together in unity, and so that the nations may come together in the peace of the Lord. This role may well cost man dearly. The way to authentic human unity is the way of self-sacrifice, for man as for God: "Greater love has no man than this, that a man lay down his life for his friends" (John 15:13). That is the legacy of man's life as he lives according to the image of the Gracious God. He is called forth from the earth, every day, to live in *agape,* as well as in *eros* and *philia.*

FROM THE VISIONS TO THE LIFESTYLE

We have tried to catch some glimpses of mankind's pilgrimage through Infinity. We have ventured into the heights and the depths of simple mystical language, with direction from the major themes of Norman O. Brown, James H. Cone, and Pierre Teilhard de Chardin, and with inspiration from the biblical apperceptions to which our tutors have pointed us. We have seen only as through a glass, darkly, but we *have* seen. We have caught sight of the contours of an enveloping and permeating cosmic process of Divine creativity, a process of life, holiness, and grace.

With this ultimate process in view, we can, it seems to me, see how everything holds together in a coherent way. On the one hand, there is the relatively tangible image of

Spaceship Earth, which entails the ideas of quality of life and social justice as well as survival, and on the other hand, the relatively tangible image of love as *eros, philia,* and *agape,* a love that is to be the valuational energy for the Spaceship. They now evidently *do* fit harmoniously together, in the greater context of the relatively intangible vision of the immediate creative activity of a God who is living, holy, and gracious.

Thus far, however, we have been concerned mainly with a kind of intellectual coherence, with the *vision* of how all things are related to each other. I do not want to deny for a moment the importance, for people such as myself, of this drive to mystical completeness. Nevertheless, the decisive side of life is not the dimension of vision (*theoria*), but the dimension of practice (*praxis*). What counts, when all has been said, is not so much whether we can hold together the Spaceship model and the three forms of love in our thinking, but whether we can embody them in our living.

Chapter Three

An Ecstatic
Lifestyle

To an increasing number of persons interested in the eco-logical crisis, a new lifestyle means such things as buying lead-free gasoline, saving newspapers for recycling, writing letters to congressmen opposing the Alaskan pipeline, and planting new trees. Such activities are not to be disparaged, but they fall far short of the kind of lifestyle required for life on the coming Spaceship Earth.

What is required is nothing less than a total transforma-tion of the lifestyle to which we have grown accustomed. What is required is *ecstasy,* which literally means "standing outside of" oneself. We must learn how to stand outside of the patterns of life that we have inherited and that we take for granted. We must learn how to be beside ourselves: *to be beside ourselves with love.* Life on the good Spaceship Earth will require a style of life that is a living embodiment of *eros, philia,* and *agape.* The competitive, manipulative, consump-tive American pattern of "business as usual" must be quickly brought to an end. Without delay we must create a new universal pattern of life as love.

What is this ecstatic style of life to be concretely? How are we to stand outside of our present pattern of life? How are we to be beside ourselves with love? I propose that we think of the new lifestyle for the good Spaceship Earth as a living interrelationship connecting the major dimensions of the human life cycle: childhood, adolescence, and adulthood. This dynamic kind of pattern can provide us with a tangible and intelligible personal orientation that embodies the various aspects of love we have identified as essential in our review of the perspectives of Norman O. Brown, James H. Cone, and Pierre Teilhard de Chardin.

Childhood—*eros.* Adolescence—*philia.* Adulthood—*agape.* These are the personal elements of the new ecstatic lifestyle. No single element of these three will suffice by itself. To accept only one would be a sign of immaturity. All three will function together. These elements are *dimensions* of a person's life, in other words, not stages. They are simultaneous aspects, not temporal periods. At various times and places, to be sure, one or two of these dimensions may or should predominate. But if one's style of life is to be truly ecstatic, if a person is truly to stand outside of himself in love, all of these dimensions must be present to one degree or another. And, of course, they *can* be! This much we have been taught by Erik Erikson's psychological studies of personal growth.[1] A truly mature person, in Erikson's psychological perspective, brings essential elements—such as basic trust and moral earnestness—from earlier stages of life. So analogously from a religious perspective, I want to suggest that an ecstatic style of life means existentially uniting the dimensions of childhood, adolescence, and adulthood. In this way our lives can be shaped by love—*eros, philia,* and *agape*—and we can live and walk by that holistic, realistic kind of love as we join together in our pilgrimage through Infinity.

LIVING LIKE A CHILD

According to the teaching of Jesus, one cannot enter the Kingdom of God unless one becomes as a little child. Let us

1. See, for example, Erik Erikson, *Childhood and Society* (New York: W. W. Norton, 1950).

reflect upon what that statement might mean concretely. We can hastily say what it does not mean. It does not mean being childish. It does not mean neurotic dependence on some arbitrary external authority. No, being like a child is to open oneself to the primordial elements of life, to enter into what Paul Tillich called the dimension of depth.

To live as a child, first of all, means *to be,* to rest from one's labors. "Come unto me all you who labor, and I will give you rest." The child lives within a framework that allows him to attend simply to the immediate moment. His activities are defined by basic trust.

Once, during the course of his ministry, Martin Luther had preached a rousing sermon on a saint's day, and had urged his congregation to redouble their efforts to be disciples of the Lord. Later in the day a member of the parish came into the local tavern only to see the great Dr. Luther sitting there with some friends imbibing heavily. "But Dr. Luther," the startled man asked, "after a sermon like that, how can you just sit here?" Luther replied: "As I drink my Wittenberg beer, the Gospel runs its course." A childlike naiveté! And perhaps a paradigm for us today: knowing how *to be,* knowing how to rest. Note, most assuredly, that being and resting do not mean copping out. Call them a "lifestyle moratorium," although that expression leaves something to be desired. To be and to rest, in any case, is not to drop out, but to pause along the way.

And more. It is not the pause of exhaustion, although physical sleep can surely be a beautiful thing in the eyes of the Lord. Children surely need lots of it. No, the pause is much more a pause for the carefree life, for playfulness, for celebration, for festivity and fantasy. Time to dream. Time to feast on all manner of good things. Time to take joy in the little things. In keeping with the childlike trust depicted by Jesus: "Consider the lilies of the field, how they grow; they neither toil nor spin; yet I tell you, even Solomon in all his glory was not arrayed like one of these. But if God so clothes the grass of the field, which today is alive and tomorrow is thrown into the oven, will he not much more clothe you, O men of little faith?" (Mt. 6:28ff.) As children, we are not to be anxious about such things as food and clothing and shelter, as we pause along the way.

Next to the teaching of Jesus, I suppose the richest source of teaching about the childlike dimension today, is to be found in the world of that award-winning children's television program, *Sesame Street*. A typical sequence goes like this: Ralph and Trudy Monster, two puppets, appear on a TV giveaway show called "You Win Your Life." Ralph is already identified as one who has a passion for eating cookies. It turns out that Ralph and Trudy Monster answer all the questions correctly. Guy Smiley, the announcer, tells them that they can have one of two prizes: *either* an all-expense-paid trip to Hawaii, a new house, and $10,000 in cash, *or*—a cookie. Ralph and Trudy deliberate, and choose the cookie! Everyone applauds joyously.

In our age of compulsive accumulation of material gadgets and goods—the garish trip-to-Hawaii mind-set—*Sesame Street* may be one of our few hopes left. To know how to choose a cookie, instead of the grossness of the American national product! That is part of what it means to live like a child. To choose consciously the life of voluntary austerity, and to enjoy it.

The child will have his joyous feasts, to be sure, as he pauses along the way. But those feasts will, in all likelihood, be meals of ice cream and cookies in a room decorated with inexpensive crepe paper, or sandwiches in a sack for that glorious meal in the hidden places of the woods. The child need not drive into the city to have a gourmet meal in an air-conditioned penthouse restaurant in order to feast.

Also, in contrast to the dominant Puritan patterns of industrial society, the child will as a matter of course be in close touch with the vitalities of his body and the wonders of nature. My little daughter loves to walk around the house without any clothes on, and loves to look at flowers in the yard. This theme reminds me again of Luther's remark that the greatest glory of Adam and Eve before the fall was that they walked about naked. Nudity, we might say, within a context of childlike carefreeness, is next to godliness.[2] This was one of the messages of the recently popular rock musical *Hair* (although the production I saw was awfully serious and mechanical, hardly carefree), and is being brought to our attention generally today by many who identify with the "counter-culture," the flower children, and others. And rightly so.

In this connection—dare I suggest it?—the child will jettison this compulsive—and consumptive—American deodorant mentality: dye the hair, paint the face, hold in the buttocks, lift up the breasts, sanitize the mouth, whiten the teeth, and make sure that you have sweet smelling feet, etc. For a child, the body *as it is given* is beautiful and totally enjoyable.

The child, moreover, is one who *walks,* who uses his legs rather than allowing them to atrophy in an automobile. The child bicycles from here to there and is not turned off, unless he is taught to be, by mildly inclement weather. The child uses his body by exercising, by running and bending and dancing. "I jump joyful jumble along," says the song of *Sesame Street.* The child is a bodily creature.

The child also knows how to wonder: to consider the lilies of the field; to ponder deeply a snowflake fallen on his sleeve; to look with wide eyes of delight when the bowl of Cheerios is set in front of him; to ponder a pebble dropped from a bridge into a little stream below. Such a sense of

2. This theme is developed in an unpublished essay by Richard A. Underwood, "Eschatological Nudity: Body, Soul, and the New Sensibility," read to the New England Region of the American Academy of Religion, October 24, 1969.

wonder is closely related to a soaring fantasy life, maybe even mystical intuitions. What is the child creating when he finger paints? Maybe just patterns of color. Maybe the primordial depths of the unconscious that Norman O. Brown likes to talk about. Listen to the testimony of Nikos Kazant-zakis, who is best known for his *Zorba the Greek*. Speaking of his own life, he writes:

> When I wish to speak of the sea, woman, or God in my writing, I gaze down into my breast and listen carefully to what the child within me says. He dictates to me; and if it sometimes happens that I come close to these great forces of sea, woman, and God, approach them by means of words and depict them, I owe it to the child who still lives within me. I become a child again to enable myself to view the world always for the first time.[3]

For the child, the world is always fresh. The world is full of wonders.

In a time when the Corporate State is making more and more demands on us, subtle and not so subtle, fashioning us everyday into more perfect "one dimensional men" (Marcuse), a momentary "return to nature" *can* help us step off the technocratic treadmill. Such a return can expose us to elemental human simplicity and vitality, and so point us to a more profound kind of existence when we turn back, as we must without delay, to join the family of mankind in the milieu of technological society. When the child of nature returns to the world of adolescence and adulthood, there will be before us a tangible sign of hope and an alluring example of promise, and we will be less likely to fall into despair and fatigue in our adolescent and adult struggles in the midst of the Corporate State.

3. Nikos Kazantzakis, *Report to Greco,* tr. P. A. Bien (New York: Simon & Shuster, 1965), p. 49.

The child, we can say in summary, is one who knows how to live and to rest in *eros,* and who can attract others to do the same. The child is a sign of hope for the untrammeled life of joy. The child is one who images-forth in his life the vitality of the Living God. We desperately need to learn anew how to *be* as children.

LIVING LIKE AN ADOLESCENT

If the characteristic marks of the child are being and resting in joy, the characteristic marks of the adolescent are acting and protesting with passion. Whereas the child pauses along the way, without a care, to play and to wonder, the adolescent—typically with his peers and usually full of cares —assumes a position of apartness, in order to gain perspective and to engage himself in the process of changing conditions on the road. Whereas the child is shaped most directly by the id and by *eros,* as he indulges himself in a feast of life, the adolescent is shaped most directly by the superego and by *philia.* The adolescent is passionately concerned with justice, with the brotherhood and sisterhood of mankind.

Obviously, we are here dealing with a type, just as we were when we considered the child. In practice, adolescents can be as childish as children sometimes are. Nothing showed this more clearly than the months following the nationwide student strikes in the Spring of 1970. There was a national orgy of action and protest on our campuses. When this orgy did not immediately produce the desired results, many adolescents across the land (and many adults as well) took their dolls and went home. Notwithstanding such acts of childishness, I want very much to highlight adolescence as an essential moment of the new ecstatic lifestyle.

The adolescent is profoundly committed to the political order and to justice within that order. He has a deep store of moral passion that energizes his life. And no group or institution is too large or too entrenched to discourage him.

He is a protestant in the historical sense of that term. If need be, he will take on the Pope and burn his decrees, as Luther did. If need be, he will seek to dump President Lyndon Johnson and will burn his draft cards. If need be, he will disrupt the machinery of a polluting industry. He will be willing to topple whole institutions, or see them radically reformed, for justice's sake. He will not be bought off by sweet words and promises. He will demand action and results. The adolescent, we can imagine, will work with his peers to change the course of society immediately. His is a sense of urgency. Change must happen right away.

The adolescent has a particularly important role to play today within the context of the ecology movement. There is a great danger that as the crisis becomes more and more evident, enthusiasm will build for solutions that will neglect the plight of the poor and of minority groups, or even make that plight worse. A tax on a family's children in excess of two, for example, to cite one idea that has been advanced, would definitely discriminate against the poor. Likewise, *ad hoc* closings of certain polluting and resource-exhausting industries might well do untold damage to the lives of the workers and their families. Across the board investments in ecological programs by government agencies may have the same effect, if those programs are not planned with great care. In this connection, too, the cry may go out from the affluent sectors—analogous to the slogan "guns or butter" we have been hearing during the Vietnam epoch—that we cannot resolve the ecological crisis *and* make investments in genuine urban renewal at the same time.

All of these ways of using the ecology issue against the poor, the dispossessed, and the oppressed must be passionately challenged by the adolescent. This can first be undertaken by conventional means—teach-ins, letter writing campaigns, electoral and congressional politics, protest marches, etc. But it is conceivable that more radical steps will be

required, depending on the kind of response that is forth-
coming from the affluent sector of American society when it
truly begins to understand the seriousness of the crisis. Some
time ago, a group of ghetto citizens in Boston hired a garbage
truck, filled it with ghetto garbage, which, as usual, had not
been collected by the city, and dumped it on the front steps
of City Hall. Maybe the time will come when urban action
groups will decide to drive their hired garbage trucks out
into the suburbs to the steps of the Town Hall on the green
to illustrate the conditions of urban existence. Maybe the
time will come for them to capture a few city rats and
release them in a spic and span all-convenience suburban
shopping center. I mean these remarks to be taken seriously,
but not too seriously. They are meant to highlight the kind
of righteous mood and will-to-action the adolescent will
justly feel, whenever the ecology movement even so much
as *tends* to neglect the poor—even if the neglect is "benign."
More positively, the adolescent will continually and forcefully espouse the cause of *urban* ecology as an absolutely
essential dimension of the ecology movement.[4] The faces of
our cities bear the scars of decades of neglect. Services are
woeful; living conditions are depressed; buildings are insen-
sitively designed; prices are high; transportation is ineffec-
tual. Along with the theme of urban ecology, moreover, the
adolescent will regularly raise the issues of world poverty
and white racism, whenever and wherever the ecological
crisis is discussed. "Do you propose to clean up this river,"
he will ask, for example, "without supplying funds to re-
invigorate the ghetto schools and housing and playgrounds

4. I have learned a great deal in this connection from an unpublished
paper by Norman J. Faramelli, "Pollution Control And/Or Social
Justice?—Urban Ecology as the Basis of a New Alliance," distributed
by the Boston Industrial Mission, 56 Boylston Street, Cambridge,
Massachusetts, (April 1971). See also Faramelli's article, "Perilous
Links Between Economic Growth, Justice, and Ecology: A Challenge
for Economic Planners," *Environmental Affairs*, I, 1 (April, 1971),
pp. 218-227.

by which the river flows after it leaves the countryside?" "Do you propose to spend millions for feed-lot pollution abatement," he will write his Senator, "when the protein for those polluting cattle is plundered from starving people in Latin America? What programs do you propose to assure that those Latin American resources get to the hungry people in Latin America?" And so on.

Once the era of the Spaceship has begun to dawn, the adolescent will continue to function as a creative agent of group power. By his commitment and his solidarity he will continue to strive to create institutions that will offer a better living space for the child and the adult, for *eros* and *agape*. As we learned from our review of the thought of James Cone, righteous power can never be dispensed with. There will be power politics on the Spaceship, but only for the sake of creativity, not destruction. And power politics will continue to be a province of the adolescent.

Now, properly speaking, this adolescent zeal will not be zeal for zeal's sake, although sometimes in practice that is what has happened. It will emphatically be zeal for justice's sake. Hence the goal of any protest or any proposal will not be "to make a point," to get one's feelings off one's chest, but to score at least a small victory for social justice. To write letters against projects like the SST, may well be chosen instead of, let us say, dramatically storming the White House.

But the adolescent will not be content merely to act and protest against the institutions of society when they must be changed or overthrown. The adolescent will also, characteristically, work with his peers to establish *counter-institutions*. With his detachment, his sense of urgency, his social passion, and his peer solidarity, the adolescent is in a position to face this momentous kind of challenge. As Richard Barnet and Marcus Raskin point out, counter-institutions have a double function. They are "not merely experiments in solving basic problems in new ways and in confronting the established institutions with their failure." They also can be "the embodiment of new non-competitive, non-authoritarian values" and thereby can set an example for all.[5] The adolescent, in this sense, can be the innovator, the trend-setter, for society. That is to say, the rock music, the bell-bottom trousers, and the pure peanut butter that so fascinate Charles Reich are interesting, but more or less irrelevant. What is decisive is new institutions. And creating them can be the adolescent's forte.

We can think in this regard of a variety of viable counter-institutions—new schools, newspapers, health services, food cooperatives, child care centers, and automobile cooperatives. We can also think of a variety of new institutions for living together and cooperating with one another to reduce population, consume less, and to have a greater impact on the community for the sake of social justice. Here the contemporary commune movement comes to mind.

Overall there are two kinds of communes, those that are cop-out undertakings, and those that are defined to have an identifiable impact on society as a whole. Raymond Mungo's Total Loss Farm is exhibit A of the first kind.[6] In contrast, I want to highlight a project of the second kind; this is being developed by an independent "think tank," The Cambridge Institute. This group is working to develop an entirely new city, which, unlike many other so-called "new towns," will incorporate the institutions appropriate for Spaceship Earth. As the prospectus states, it will be a city—located perhaps in Vermont—that will be based on "a vision of justice, communitarian values, decentralized institutions, and planning by its own citizens." But, above all, plans are to make this city "politically cogent," that is, part of a broader strategy to move the nation as a whole. "Our strategy," the

5. Richard Barnet and Marcus Raskin, *An American Manifesto* (New York: New American Library, 1970), pp. 61ff.
6. See Raymond Mungo, *Total Loss Farm* (New York: E. P. Dutton, 1970).

prospectus explains, and then documents in some detail, "will involve every opportunity to let others see what we are doing in the new city. It will involve our moving out of the new city to educate and assist others who are interested in applying the models we have developed."[7] The new city, as it were, will have a program of foreign aid and foreign influence. It will regularly send educational and financial assistance to help develop similar cities elsewhere and seek to exert a corresponding influence at the highest levels of state and national government. The new city, in short, will definitely be a counter-institution, but with a view to moving and transforming the whole society to which it is juxtaposed; the new city stands in sharp contrast to undertakings such as Total Loss Farm, which are predicated on detachment from and denial of society at large.

Another even more ambitious example of a socially germane counter-institution is the proposal for "Centers for National Reform" put forward by Arnold Schuchter in his book *Reparations: The Black Manifesto and Its Challenge to White America*. This proposal represents a particularly vivid instance of how the adolescent mind-set, which I have been describing, might proceed to an embodiment of *philia*, love for the oppressed brother. Supported by the massive resources of American churches and synagogues, and based initially in already existing, but transformed black colleges in the southern United States, these Centers for National Reform would work to shift the priorities of American society from war and exploitation of people and the environment to peace and an ecologically sane economics of social justice. Specifically, the Centers would have the following nine major purposes, as Schuchter envisions them:

1. to prepare conversion plans and guidelines, operating as 'think-tanks' for a reparations program in a peace economy;

7. "Prospectus: A New City," Cambridge Institute (Cambridge, Mass., 1970), pp. 1, 7.

2. to watch government policies and operations that support militarization at the expense of conversion to a peace economy;

3. to educate blacks and whites in changing the dominant institutions of our society in accordance with the goals of redress, with a special focus on universities;

4. to prepare plans for new cities and towns as well as for the renewal of existing urban communities, with an initial focus on opportunities in the South;

5. to play a key role in political mobilization and education in the South aimed at accelerating black acquisition of political power;

6. to attract the largest possible number of scientists, and technicians displaced by a contracting war economy to teach in black colleges, to assist in preparing realistic conversion plans, new communities, and renewal of cities;

7. in general to upgrade dramatically the cultural and educational opportunities of black colleges, in part for the purpose of attracting talented white students committed to the goals of redress;

8. to educate clergy from all religious denominations so that they can return to their churches as missionaries for the goals of redress; and

9. to provide a setting in which whites and blacks from diverse backgrounds, from the Black Panthers to Wall Streeters, can exchange ideas on national conversion policies.[8]

The scope of Schuchter's proposal may strike the business-as-usual man of practical affairs, even the "liberal," as being too "idealistic" to be workable. But recall the present shape of our national Research and Development spending; the great bulk of expenditures are on the weapons of space technology and war, with next to nothing being allocated for the weapons of social justice and an ecologically sane peace.[9] So,

8. From the book *Reparations: The Black Manifesto and Its Challenge to White America* by Arnold Schuchter. Copyright, ©, 1970, by Arnold Schuchter. Reprinted by permission of J. B. Lippincott Company. Pp. 150 ff.

9. Peter Steinfels, "The R and D Factor," *Commonweal,* September 25, 1970, p. 478.

even without pausing to examine the merits of every detail of Schuchter's proposal, we can ask whether anything *less* than this comprehensive kind of anti-racist, pro-ecology "adolescent" proposal for a society-transforming counter-institution can begin to meet the ecological and social demands of the present and move us into the era of Spaceship Earth.

That in broad outline is the shape of the adolescent dimension of the ecstatic lifestyle required by the coming Spaceship Earth: social action, protest, and the establishment of counter-institutions, all for the sake of achieving a higher level of social justice on an ecologically sane base. Adolescence is the concrete life style embodiment of *philia*. The adolescent thus images-forth the righteousness of the Holy God, in whose image he lives and moves and has his being.

LIVING LIKE AN ADULT

We come now to the third essential moment of our new ecstatic lifestyle, adulthood. Maligned as the adult may be these days, if he is true to himself we need him. Whereas the characteristic marks of the child are being and resting, and those of the adolescent are acting and protesting, the characteristic marks of the adult are cultivating and serving, cultivating his own personal growth and serving his fellows through established channels. Whereas the child pauses along the way, without a care, to play and to wonder, and the adolescent, with his peers and full of cares, assumes a position of apartness in order to come back at society to transform it, the adult continues on the way, often by himself, doing all he can to make society function as humanely as it can and to help as many individuals along the way as he can. Whereas the child is shaped most directly by the id and by *eros,* and the adolescent is shaped primarily by the superego and *philia,* the adult is shaped chiefly by the ego and by *agape*. The adult is profoundly concerned with *good* order—not the tyrannical law and order championed today by those who fear any social change, but the kind of good order characteristic of any well-functioning ecosystem, a dynamic and interdependent kind of order.

Against Norman O. Brown and with Teilhard de Chardin, accordingly, we will affirm the intrinsic goodness of human rationality. Again, the rationality in question here is not that frequently mindless rationality of the Corporate State, but the deep rationality of someone, for example, who develops detailed plans for sensitive, organic new cities.[10] Rationality —the ego—has a depth—call it *wisdom*—that Brown entirely passes by in his justifiable quest for the erotic.

The ego can create vastly complicated, creative plans for world government. Indeed, the innermost tendency of the ego is that pressing toward world government. The ego can develop philosophies of wholeness.[11] It can govern nations, as well as groups and the self, wisely. The ego can be the philosopher king. It is potentially much more than a mere instrument that fits the self as a cog into the machine of the Corporate State. Properly, the ego knows when to govern directly and when to give way to the id or the superego. Indeed, the ego's government, when it is right, is precisely the creative and harmonious interrelationship of the requirements of the id and the superego. Without the wisdom of the ego the dimensions of childhood and adolescence would be in continual conflict with each other.

Another way of treating the same theme is to say that the dimension of adulthood is the dimension of self-discipline, the time of prayer and fasting, whereas childhood is the

10. I have in mind here, among others, the extensive writings of Lewis Mumford.

11. Most recently, for example, see René Dubos, *So Human an Animal* (New York: Charles Scribners, 1968). Towering above all others at this point, however, are the writings of Alfred North Whitehead.

dimension of playful abandon, and adolescence the dimension, mainly, of group involvement and group solidarity. The adult characteristically cultivates his own individuality, and seeks constantly to grow; he tries continually to remain aware of his limitations. The adult tends to his interiority. The adult seeks solitude. Confronted by death, the adult speculates about the meaning of life. The adult, moreover, is the transmitter of culture, that rich storehouse of experience from the past, which can lend perspective to, and facilitate, delight in the present and hope for the future.

The wisdom of the adult has many expressions, all of them shaped by an inner reality of self-giving compassion. To begin with, the adult is free in his wisdom to attend to the mundane as a way of enhancing the common good. He knows that everything cannot be transformed overnight. He realizes that many minor decisions may add up to major changes over the long run. Within the context of the ecological crisis, for example, the adult will not be above simple life-style adjustments such as saving tin cans and paper for recycling, cutting back his use of plastics and other non-biodegradable materials, or using the right kind of detergent. The adult will also feel free to experiment with relatively modest changes in community patterns, such as arranging for car pools, working for the best possible refuse disposal in a neighborhood, organizing pick-up spots for used materials, either for reuse or recycling, and similar activities. Although it is true that our society must change quickly and radically if it is to survive the ecological crisis, it remains true also that change, if it is to come, will depend in part on a frontal attack on present societal patterns of consumption and pollution by all citizens where they work and where they live.[12]

12. For discussions of individual actions of this kind, see *The Environmental Handbook,* pp. 285-311; and Greg Cailliet, Paulette Setzer, and Milton Love, *Everyman's Guide to Ecological Living* (New York: Macmillan Company, 1971).

The adult's life of wisdom, shaped by self-giving compassion, also has a special bearing on the problem of population growth. Through a process of self-examination and an assessment of world and national population trends, the adult, if he has a family, will keep the size of that family in line with the general requirements of social responsibility. Overall, this seems to mean no more than two children per family.[13] The adult will also have the maturity to take into account fears of minority groups in this context, a topic we have already considered. He will be willing to accept more exacting standards for the white affluent classes than for other groups. The adult will work, furthermore, to institute a variety of educational and informational programs concerning the population problem, in schools, churches, social clubs, and elsewhere.

But perhaps the most decisive aspect of the adult life must still be mentioned; it can be called the *politics of wisdom*. The coming Spaceship Earth will not arrive on the scene by itself. Nor will it suddenly happen upon our world overnight, through some single revolutionary event. The Spaceship will begin to be a reality only with the exercise of the most astute and sustained kind of political maneuvering. This is the unique province of the adult. This is the province of the one who knows how to be wise as a fox. The reformist, incremental politics of adulthood provide an essential practical balance for the necessarily extravagant, radical politics of adolescence. Meaningful political change requires this dual political thrust. Substantive change will frequently be initiated by the adolescent. That is one of his essential tasks. Yet we will not survive on this earth, and even less will we thrive in justice, without the adult commitment to

13. This is a complex problem, as I have already indicated. The advocates of "Zero Population Growth," that is, not more than two children per two parents, seem to have a forceful argument. But this discussion is by no means closed. Without too much difficulty one can begin to think of legitimate exceptions to the rule of two children per family.

carry through with that change and to make it an integral part of the socio-political system.[14]

As in other contexts, the overall motivating force of the adult politics of wisdom, is self-giving compassion. The adult so loves the world that he incarnates himself in its structures, to be a servant to the wounded and the lonely—*to make the system work as it should*. This means much more than merely meeting one's payroll or casting a ballot. It means striving, with all the grace that one can receive, to allow the intrinsic God-given goodness of political structures to come to the fore, in a context where egocentric men obscure that goodness, sometimes to the point where it is scarcely evident. The adult is not wedded to the stability of any given political system. His focus is rather on the human dimensions of the given system. The adult, properly and importantly, is continually open to political change, however much he may serve as a point of continuity with the past. Indeed, as I have indicated, it rightfully falls to the adult to respond to the adolescent's righteous protests with detailed political programs, and to seek to adopt, in part or in whole, the adolescent's experimental counter-institutions for the whole society.

Concretely, the adult politics of wisdom has many facets. Individually it means that the adult is sensitive to the treatment of persons within a corporation or a government, and

14. Cf. the remarks of Philip E. Slater, *The Pursuit of Loneliness: American Culture at the Breaking Point* (Boston: Beacon Press, 1970), pp. 123ff.: "Change can take place only when liberal and radical pressures are both strong. Intelligent liberals have always recognized the debt they owe to radicals, whose existence permits liberals to push further than they would otherwise have dared, all the while posing as compromisers and mediators. Radicals, however, have been somewhat less sensible of their debt to liberals, partly because of the rather single-minded discipline radicals are almost forced to maintain. . . . Yet liberal adjustments often do much to soften up an initially rigid *status quo*—creating just those rising expectations that make revolutionary change possible. . . . Liberal reform and radical change are thus complementary rather than antagonistic. Together they make it possible continually to test the limits of what can be done."

that he is also aware of the effects such systems have on people beyond their boundaries. The need for this kind of individual adult politics is especially pronounced today. Charles Reich has aptly emphasized the fact that evil today is very much "the product of our system of organization and our technology, and it occurs because personal responsibility and personal awareness have been obliterated by a system deliberately designed to do just that—eliminate or minimize the human element and insure the supremacy of the system."[15] Reich mentions as an example the invention, production, and use of napalm. Nowhere along the line is any single person "really responsible" for the havoc and pain napalm has brought into the lives of Vietnamese villagers. The adult will rightfully be ready to stand up against this deadly kind of systemic "innocence" by an act of conscience. In this instance the adult naturally moves toward a coalition with the adolescent, rather than merely responding to the latter's protests. Individually, in other words, the adult is prepared to take a moral stance against the functioning of the given system when it tramples on human life. In this respect the *opposite* extreme of the responsible adult is symbolized by the still memorable figure of the efficient executioner, Adolf Eichmann, who merely "did his duty" as he sent countless thousands of Jews to their deaths.

Individually also, the adult will immerse himself in what can be called conventional politics, educating himself about the issues, talking to his friends, writing letters, making financial contributions to sound candidates for political office, and voting—all with a constant eye on the issues of ecology and justice. This kind of conventional politics also has a somewhat unconventional place in the context of the many vast quasi-governmental "private" organizations in our society. General Motors, to cite the most striking example, is a

15. Charles Reich, "Reflections: The Limits of Duty," *The New Yorker,* June 19, 1971, p. 52.

corporation whose yearly receipts are larger than those of all but two nations on this planet, the United States and the Soviet Union. There is an important place for individual adult politics within structures such as GM; for example, pressing for the design and manufacture of less polluting automobiles or for vehicles that will last a decade, rather than ones that fall prey to planned obsolescence after two years. What holds true for firms like GM also holds true for educational systems. Adult politics must flourish inside these institutions. There is a desperate need, for example, for curricula that adequately represent the ecological crisis and that instill in students a meaningful kind of ecological sensitivity. One can think here, as well, of the mass media. Considerable potential for sound ecological education is to be found here.[16] Adult politics must also be practiced in our gigantic religious institutions. I can imagine, for example, an important movement developing *to abolish the practice of buying countless Christmas gifts* (which is the prime cultic-religious sanctification of our compulsive American consumerism). Why not establish a pattern of giving hand-made gifts that might be fashioned out of materials around the home? Moreover, churches and synagogues can regularly use recycled paper and serve as centers for the collection of discarded goods for recycling. A few well-invested individual efforts could easily get such projects underway. Overall, these are some of the contours of an adult politics of wisdom, insofar as they can be set in motion by the individual acting by himself.

But the adult politics of wisdom by no means comes to an end at this point. In the American context the adult can also function fruitfully as a member of various voluntary associations, particularly those oriented toward the issues of

16. One such undertaking is a program called the "Eighth Day" seen in Seattle, Washington. Five universities in the area, sparked by an urban clergyman, Robert K. Menzel, and joined by a local TV station, produced an eight week series on ecology and arranged for people to gather to discuss it in over 400 locations.

ecology and social justice. These citizens' groups can have an impact for ecological sanity and justice in cases where single individuals would be mainly, if not totally, ineffective. Again, the adult's goal is to allow the intrinsic goodness of the given system, however distorted that system may be, to come to the fore. Citizens' groups can effectively press for meaningful legislation, testify at hearings, and engage in various forms of lobbying. They can bring lawsuits against polluters. They can organize referenda. They can organize grass roots pressure on legislators. Much of this, it bears repeating, can and should focus on the great corporate "private" structures of America, as well as on the government. A church body, for example, can have a significant voice in corporation politics, in virtue of the stock it owns, if only it develops some political sagacity. Citizens' groups can also organize selective buying campaigns aimed at putting pressure on ecologically and socially irresponsible industries to change their policies.

Perhaps the least exciting, but one of the most effective tools of citizens' groups, is research. Mere facts, if they are properly communicated, can have a political force all their own. The work of Ralph Nader is well known in this regard. But Nader is not alone. One of the most impressive instances of the power of research, and the way to develop it, is the case of Alice Tepper, a young woman a few years out of college, who founded the Council on Economic Priorities in New York City. This group, funded by small contributions and served by many consultants at no cost, does highly detailed and painstaking research on the records and policies of various industries. Its areas of interest are minority hiring, environmental responsibility, and military production. One of its most celebrated achievements was a documented study of the efforts (if any) of the country's 24 largest paper and pulp industries to fight pollution. Among other things, this study identified many plants that could be legislatively compelled to invest in pollution control operations that would not force them to shut down or relocate. Who wants to throw workers out of their jobs? Alice Tepper's exhaustive adult study undercut the kind of blanket excuse that those interested in ecological sanity frequently hear from industrial polluters. Tepper's study also revealed hard data for selective buying (it is much more responsible to buy Kleenex tissue than Scott, for example, in view of Kleenex's much better record on pollution control).

Given the power and the diffusion of the institutions of the Corporate State, however, it seems likely that the work of any citizens' group by itself will not be enough, just as the political involvement of any individual adult will not be enough. It seems likely that if American society is to change radically and soon, as it must, citizens' groups must band together to form a huge coalition: peace groups, labor unions, urban based groups, ecology groups, student organizations, various interested liberal factions of political parties, and so on. It appears that meaningful change will not be wrought unless a political force is developed that is large enough and powerful enough to rival the force of the much discussed Military-Industrial Complex and other less discussed conglomerates, such as the Automobile-Highway-Oil complex.[17] This will be a momentous undertaking. But the reality of the present political situation seems to make such a gigantic adult project unavoidable.

This context—a new Urban-Peace-Ecological complex— will probably also be the most fruitful one in which to raise the question, and to begin to move toward some kind of planetary government, or at least world wide political cooperation. It will take all the political power an Urban-Peace-Ecological complex can muster to begin to overcome the

17. I am depending here on Max Stackhouse's analysis in *The Ethics of Necropolis: An Essay on the Military Industrial Complex and the Quest for a Just Peace* (Boston: Beacon Press, 1970), Chaps. 2, 3, 4.

inertia of certain hyper-nationalistic strata in American society. Nevertheless, a world society is one of the most important priorities on the adult agenda today.[18] Such a society would be able to establish the conditions in which there could be meaningful control of arms, pollution, and resource depletion, along with a rational planetary population policy, and an international program encouraging the redistribution of wealth. This is an immense idea, obviously. But the adult is committed to long-term self-giving in politics—which is what will be required if the requisite world society is ever to come into being.

It goes without saying that the dimension of adulthood as I have depicted it here, like the dimensions of childhood and adolescence, is a *type*, an ideal representation. In practice, as everyone knows, many adults find it very easy to be very childish, to call for law and order at any price and to make every effort to rule out the life of childlike playfulness. But the adult I have in mind is the adult who is shaped by a vision such as that of Teilhard de Chardin. The adult is one who knows how to live—and die—in *agape*. The adult is one who sees himself as an expression of a universal process of reconciliation. The adult is one who images-forth the self-giving compassion of the Gracious God, in whose image he is created.

These are the three dimensions of the new ecstatic lifestyle I think the Spaceship Earth requires. These are the lifestyle elements that will allow us to step outside the patterns of life to which we have grown accustomed, patterns that have now taken us to the brink of catastrophe. These elements are not stages, as I stressed at the outset. They are a *life process*,

18. A small step in this direction, with a strong ecological emphasis, has already been taken by the American Movement for World Government, New Canaan, Conn. This group has promulgated a "Declaration of Interdependence," which is eminently worth discussion (it is printed in the New York Times, July 4, 1971, p. E5). See further the study by Richard A. Falk, *op. cit.*, chaps. V-X, for an overview of the problems and potential of a move toward world government.

a dynamic interrelationship of personal commitments, feelings, and actions. Now one will predominate in a person's life, now another. Perhaps one dimension will set the major tone in a person's life for a period of years and then give way to another. Perhaps that dimension will be dominant only for a few hours. But each of the three dimensions will constantly be "in the wings," and each will constantly be shaping, though perhaps only in hidden ways, the expressions of the other two.

As a matter of course, moreover, individuals who find their lives shaped mainly by one dimension, for however long, will coalesce and support each other. At the same time, however, an overall pattern of *interdependence* will still be evident. Properly, no group of children, adolescents, or adults, will ever live and work together without taking cognizance of, and relating creatively to, the life and work of other groups. This, then, is a *declaration of interdependence* for the area of lifestyle, both within an individual's own life and within the relationship between various groupings of children, adolescents, and adults.

In this way, in the tangible shape of an ecstatic lifestyle, the universal value of love, and particularly the visions of love as *eros*, *philia*, and *agape*, as seen respectively by Norman O. Brown, James H. Cone, and Pierre Teilhard de Chardin, will be concretely embodied. One unified ecstatic lifestyle will emerge as the value-input into the Spaceship model. Living as a child, as an adolescent, and as an adult, a person's life will be a dynamic process of love as he joins with others in the same process. This will make the Spaceship not only a reality, but a beautiful place to live. It will make it a brilliantly shining reflection of the Divine Milieu in which it is moving. The whole Spaceship will image-forth the life, the holiness, and the grace of the ultimate creative process, which envelops it and permeates it, as it holds a steady course in its pilgrimage.

Chapter Four

The Church as Matrix
of the New Lifestyle

How is a new ecstatic lifestyle to be developed and sustained and deepened? How is an international congregation of citizens who are ready for life on the Spaceship to come into being? The answer must be this: *today those who are concerned with the new ecstatic lifestyle must be in touch with each other, gather together, and covenant with each other to form a global community of mutual support.* It is an ecological principle that everything is related to everything else. So it seems highly unlikely that any single individual or isolated group will be able successfully to rise above the given system and develop a lifestyle that is appropriate for a system that has yet to be born. So new international communities must come into being; communities that will help their members shape their lives according to the new ecstatic lifestyle. A single pine tree may well fall to the elements. A group of pine trees will probably flourish in the protection they provide each other. So each one who is seeking to develop the new ecstatic lifestyle must, I am convinced, seek out an international community, or seek to develop such a community, with that kind of orientation.

Here the particularity of my own stance will be especially evident. I look to the *Church* to be the fertile soil where I may seek to grow into the new lifestyle. I do not want to deny that there may well be other patches of fertile soil for other people. I simply have found one that looks good to me, and that I have come to depend on. This is how this particular community of support looks to me, in broad outline: as the matrix of the new lifestyle, the Church has a ministry that is threefold—priestly, prophetic, and pastoral. These aspects of the Church's ministry are the fertile soil for the elements of the new life style, the moments of childhood, adolescence, and adulthood.

In so far as the Church is *priestly*, it celebrates the presence of God in Christ. It considers the lilies of the field, how they toil not. It rests in the vitality of the Divine Presence. It becomes as a little child in order to enter the Kingdom of God. It sings songs of joy and praise as it gathers together, and as it disperses throughout the world. It presents its bodies as a living sacrifice to God.

In so far as the Church is *prophetic*, it participates urgently and wholeheartedly in the struggle for human liberation, whatever form that may take. It stands over against the inherited order, when that order is found wanting, and calls for social justice. It organizes itself to lend support, financially and bodily, to the oppressed peoples of the world. It becomes the rich young ruler in the Gospel of Luke, only the story has a different ending; the Church does *not* because of its riches turn sadly away from Jesus and his call for discipleship. On the contrary, the Church gives up its capital in order to follow Jesus. The Church seeks first the Kingdom of God and his righteousness. It identifies itself with the righteous power of God.

In so far as the Church is *pastoral* it tends to the needs of all individuals, but especially, like the good Samaritan, to those who are fallen by the wayside. The Church characteristically leaves the ninety-nine secure sheep and seeks out the one who is lost. Its members call each other by name, moreover, and they seek to call every individual they encounter by name. Though the noise of world history may be loud indeed, the Church's ears are always attuned to hear those little ones who are alone, who are hungry, who are in prison. Within the structures of the world the Church attends to the human dimension. It seeks to embody the self-giving compassion of God.

Concretely, in the matrix of this priestly, prophetic, and pastoral ministry, I find the kind of resources I think I need to develop an ecstatic lifestyle, with its moments of childhood, adolescence, and adulthood. I hasten to add that, like many other people today, I have experienced a number of "bad trips" in the Church. It scarcely needs to be observed that the American Church in particular has sold out in many ways to that competitive, manipulative, consumptive American pattern of business-as-usual. What is remarkable—and it is this to which I am testifying from personal experience— is that here and there and indeed everywhere little patches of fertile soil can be seen, where the Church *is* being the Church and not (to slightly change an old joke) "the Corporate State at prayer." I know people who know how to live like children, like adolescents, and like adults, who know how to embody *eros* and *philia* and *agape. This* is the Church I am referring to.

JESUS CHRIST AS THE WHOLENESS OF THE CHURCH

Further, to me the Church is not just the sum of its parts. The whole of this living mystical Body is greater than the sum of its parts. This element of wholeness can be identified with a variety of images. For me, the element of wholeness is the living cosmic Christ. Ultimately, in my own perspective, it is he who holds the Church together and it is he who, like the sun shining on fertile soil, makes possible the Church's priestly, prophetic, and pastoral ministry.[1]

1. This discussion of Christ, it will be evident, is only a single brush stroke. Much more would have to be painted in were the whole picture to begin to do justice to the reality it seeks to depict. For more details, see my *Brother Earth,* chap. VIII.

Christ is the *life-giver*. He is the incarnate risen Lord who claims our bodies for the resurrection, and with them the whole natural order. He is the beginning, the first manifestation, of the new heavens and the new earth. He is the host at the cosmic banquet of joy, which is the consummation of this universe. In his presence the lamb and the lion play together, and a little child shall lead them. He is the gentle Lord who sanctifies childhood as the way into the Kingdom of God.

Christ is the *just judge*. He himself embodies the prophetic protest against injustice when, according to John, He drives the money changers out of the temple with a whip. He himself embodies the adolescent style when He claims not to bring peace, but a sword, when he says he has come to set a man against his father and a daughter against her mother. He is the Lord of righteousness who has come to set men free.

Christ is the *self-giving reconciler*. He comes in the form of weakness to seek out the lost sheep. He befriends tax collectors, prostitutes, and lepers. He mediates healing to the sick. He preaches good news to the poor. Finally, totally alone and in the hands of corrupt powers, he offers himself on the cross for the sake of the many. On the cross he asks forgiveness for his persecutors. His life and death are the perfect embodiment of the self-giving love of adulthood.

LITURGY AS THE HALLUCINOGEN

The question still can be asked, however, and rightly so, how does one "turn on" to this Christ and his mystical Body? —if that is what one is inclined to do. What does one do in order to hallucinate christically and to find support for that kind of hallucination in the Body of the Church?

To see portents of ecological catastrophe these days is not all that difficult. One need only read some books and attend a few ecology rallies. One need only hear the word from the ecological prophets of doom such as Barry Commoner or Paul Ehrlich.[2] Nowadays, once one has begun to look, it does not take much work or imagination to see the blood-dimmed tide. Signs of it can be seen by anyone who has eyes to see. But how does one go about seeing the vision of the dearest freshness deep down things?

For those, many or few, who want to be able to hope for a new heavens and a new earth, a new world latent in that dearest freshness deep down things, and who want to have that hope begotten and nurtured by the risen cosmic Christ and his mystical Body, I have a suggestion. For those, many or few, who have this kind of openness to classical Christian symbols and to the community that bears those symbols, or who think they may be moving toward that kind of openness, I want to make a proposal. Try letting the liturgy function as your hallucinogen. See if the ritual of the Church, when it is authentic, can turn you on to the dearest freshness.

In his instructive article on ritual, Erikson points out that ritual behavior is the concrete mode of psychological identity development.[3] For example, the mutual smiles of recognition when the parent comes into the young child's room in the morning reenforce the child's "basic trust" and help to alleviate the parent's anxieties. In a similar way, I think we can say that *ritual is the concrete mode of identity formation in the mystical Body of Christ*. By going through these particular motions, when they are right, one can learn how to hallucinate christically and thereby how to live ecstatically in the matrix of the Church.

I am aware that much of the Church's ritual today is dull. Indeed, in mainstream Christianity today so much of the

2. Barry Commoner, *Science and Survival* (New York: Viking Press, 1963); Paul Ehrlich, *The Population Bomb* (New York: Ballantine Books, 1968).
3. Erik H. Erikson, "The Development of Ritualization," in *The Religious Situation: 1968,* ed. Donald R. Cutler (Boston: Beacon Press, 1968), pp. 711-733.

vitality, the relevance, and the sensitivity has been squeezed out of the liturgy in so many instances that one can wonder whether God has not decided to breathe his creative Spirit into some other atmosphere. Much Christian worship in America, moreover, seems to be perfectly constructed to turn out well-lubricated citizens of the Corporate State. But this kind of critique of mainstream Christianity is a familiar story. What bears saying here is that it does not have to be that way, and that, as a matter of fact, it is not that way everywhere.

Liturgy properly is *childlike*. It is the play of the children of God, who have come together saying "Abba" (Father). Accordingly, liturgy is full of action. You *do* things when you worship. You play. You prance around bodily. You do not just sit there in your place and listen, maybe standing occasionally to sing. You get into the act bodily, offering your body to God as a living sacrifice. How can we live as children, as the new ecological age requires, if our worship lacks the element of bodily movement? We would be schizoid: seeking during the week to be bodily creatures, but being shaped on Sundays by a hyper-spiritual kind of worship.

As you move around playfully, moreover, you are celebrating. The Spirit enlivens your mortal bodies to dance for joy and to speak in tongues. Celebrating and dancing, you gather around the Lord's Table, and feast together, partaking of his cosmic banquet mystically. You eat the bread and drink the wine of the new creation, and you begin to turn on to a vision of universal proportions and to a joy that expands your consciousness and excites your viscera. You fantasize with your fellows about the new heavens and the new earth. And, as you touch each other's flesh, embracing one another with the kiss of peace, you begin to sense the dearest freshness deep down things. For this moment, the cares of the world have been set aside by the sweetness of your dream. For this moment the agonizing work that lies before you is not on your mind. You are resting in a community of life, being upheld faithfully in the arms of the living cosmic Christ.

A group of friends and I were at the shore, way out on the tip of Cape Cod, just at the point where Thoreau said one can stand and have the whole of America behind him. The sensuous sand cliffs towered behind us, a hot warming sun burned overhead, and the deep cold blue of the summer Atlantic crashed on the beach in front of us, sending forth brilliant flashes of white salty water. Under my prostrate body, lying face down with no blanket and no bathing suit to separate me anywhere from a million variegated granules of warming sand, my brother the earth was full of caresses. When the right time had come, we were standing up and running toward the water. There, after the initial cold shock, buoyed up by the salt water, I floated on my back in another world, looking up at the sun with blinded joyful eyes. That is what the Church's ritual is like, when it is right. That is the liturgical dimension of childlike trust and play and sensuous joy.

Liturgy also is properly a ritual embodiment of the dimension of *adolescence*. Liturgy has its moments of prophetic protest. This especially comes to the fore in the preaching of the Word of God. The sermon ought to have an incarnational thrust. It ought to be shaped by the example of Jesus' own life. Thus Jesus did not just teach about love, he acted it out. He ministered to the poor. He drove the money changers out of the temple. So sermons will, with regular cadence, be addressed to the situation of poverty and oppression. And those who preach will not merely speak of love, they will show what they are preparing to do to act out that love, and they will invite their hearers to do the same.

The congregation will then actively respond to this prophetic message. Maybe there will be a time for "community concerns" in the liturgy, when the people of Christ can talk and debate and organize action or at least agree when they are going to meet to do that. Then the congregation will sing militant hymns of discipleship and utter fervent prayers for guidance.

Liturgy is impoverished without this prophetic, adolescent dimension. We should keep this in mind when news stories attempt to impress us with accounts of the back-to-Jesus movement: the "Jesus freaks," *Jesus Christ Superstar*, and all the rest. The Jesus who is depicted in the Gospels calls us to seek the Kingdom of God *and* his righteousness. He does not tell us to be dropouts. Maybe, remembering the perspective of James Cone, the best way to put this is to say that it is beautiful to be turned on by the ritual of the Church, but make sure that ritual is, in addition to everything else, a celebration of blackness. Liturgy, when it is right, always contains within it the dimension of passionate adolescent protest for the sake of social justice.

Finally, liturgy is properly the ritual embodiment of the dimension of *adulthood*. Liturgy properly has its deeply serious moments of quiet—cathedral solitude. These are the times for the humble prayers and petitions of the faithful, some of which they may not even know how to utter. These are the times when each one can acknowledge his own struggle for faith, saying "I believe, Lord; help my unbelief." The child plays joyfully. The adolescent gets involved passionately with the renewal of the world. For the adult the liturgy offers the time to identify and deal with the dark night of the soul, to search for wisdom and insight, to hope to see through a glass darkly rather than not to see at all: to say, "My God, my God, why hast thou forsaken me?," to give the Lord no rest, crying out for him to hasten the day of his Kingdom, to ask him for daily bread.

Paradoxically, this adult struggle for faith comes to its apex in the Church's confession of faith, in the hymns and in the creeds. For here the holy catholic faith is confessed, by the whole congregation. Only the whole congregation can confess the faith truly! Each one of us will probably always have his or her difficulties, his or her blind spots. So when we join together in confessing the faith we are at the same time acknowledging our own inability to confess by ourselves.

Another distinctive element of the adult dimension of the liturgy is the growth of personal and interpersonal sensitivity. This has been present in the ritual of the Church for a long time, although the contemporary movement of Sensitivity Training can serve as a helpful reminder of this element if some have forgotten it. Luther referred to this as "the mutual consolation of the brethren." You *know* those who worship with you. You miss them when for one reason or another they are not present. You feel with them, when they are despondent. You rejoice with them when they are happy. This element comes to the fore liturgically especially in the eucharistic prayer. Here the whole congregation remembers Mrs. Jones, whose son is missing in Vietnam. Here the whole congregation is with an unnamed friend who is going through a mental breakdown. Here the whole congregation gives powerful thanks to the Lord for Janet's and Mike's newly adopted son. The prayers of the Church at its liturgical highpoint, at the apex of its central ritual, have this kind of personal concreteness. And this concreteness, as a matter of course, is reflected in the conversations between the members before, during, and following the Service.

So that is what the liturgy is, when it is right. Liturgy is the hallucinogen. Liturgy is the ritual embodiment of the ecstatic lifestyle. Liturgy is going through the motions of identity formation in the mystical Body of Christ. Liturgy is the intramural side of the Church's priestly, prophetic, and pastoral ministry. Liturgy is how to get in touch with the risen cosmic Christ, his vitality, his righteousness, and his reconciliation. Liturgy is learning to live in love, in *eros*, *philia*, and *agape*. Liturgy is learning to live as a child, as an adolescent, and as an adult.

With the Hope that
the End is the Beginning

Here ends, in these very particular personal terms, my report on my visions. But I do not want things to end here. I ask the reader point blank: where do you stand and what do you think? I hope this end point is just a beginning for you. I invite you now to dream your own dreams, not just the nightmares, but also the visions of peace and justice and ecological sanity. I invite you to dream—for the sake of our survival, for the sake of our humanity.

DATE DUE

FEB 14 '89			
MAR 4 '91			
FEB 28 '92			